Living By the Seat of My Pants!
Inspirational Exploits, Splinters and All

*To Haki Mi Cloud —
With best wishes.
Edmund C Hughes
3/2/03*

Edmund C. Hughes
Lieutenant Colonel, Infantry
AUS (Retired Reserve)

Book design, graphics and typesetting: Roy Diment,
Vivencia Resources Group. www.members.shaw.ca/vrg

National Library of Canada Cataloguing in Publication

Hughes, Edmund C
   Living by the seat of my pants / Edmund C. Hughes.

ISBN 1-55369-458-9

   1. Hughes, Edmund C. 2. Journalists--United States--Biography. 3. World War, 1939-1945--Campaigns--Pacific Area. 4. World War, 1939-1945--Personal narratives, American. 5. World War, 1939-1945--Journalists--Biography. 6. War correspondents--United States--Biography. I. Title.

PN4874.H76A3 2002   070.92   C2002-901909-5

 *PRINTED IN CANADA*

This book was published *on-demand* in cooperation with Trafford Publishing.
On-demand publishing is a unique process and service of making a book available for retail sale to the public taking advantage of on-demand manufacturing and Internet marketing.
On-demand publishing includes promotions, retail sales, manufacturing, order fulfilment, accounting and collecting royalties on behalf of the author.

Suite 6E, 2333 Government St., Victoria, B.C. V8T 4P4, CANADA
Phone   250-383-6864   Toll-free   1-888-232-4444 (Canada & US)
Fax   250-383-6804   E-mail   sales@trafford.com
Web site   www.trafford.com   TRAFFORD PUBLISHING IS A DIVISION OF TRAFFORD HOLDINGS LTD.
Trafford Catalogue #02-0271   www.trafford.com/robots/02-0271.html

10   9   8   7   6   5   4   3

Dedication

With Deepest Love
To
My Wife, **Eunice McGriff Hughes**
Without Whose Devotion and Understanding
This Book Would Never Have Been Written
Also
With Loving Pride
To
My Children
(In order of their appearance)
**Elizabeth Corrie Barrett, Edmund Jackson Hughes,
Lee Ann Finger**
and
My Eight Grandchildren and Seven Great Grandchildren

With God's Blessings
May They Live Long, Multiply and Prosper

ACKNOWLEDGMENTS

With deep appreciation, I wish to acknowledge the help and encouragement extended by several friends and colleagues.

First, I am indebted to **Forrest Wallace Cato**, highly competent author and editor, for the invaluable assistance he rendered. Wally, knowing how to inspire and motivate, gave me hope and encouragement during some of my most trying times. He also prodded me to resume writing after an extended period of inactivity due to that dreaded breakdown that afflicts all of us at times — inertia.

Then, there's **Mac McCoin**, long-time friend now living in Knoxville, Tenn., who has given unsparingly of time and effort in critiquing and polishing my less than perfect prose. Mac has written several highly-readable novels, and has hopes of one being published soon.

John Post, staunch friend and supporter for many years dating back to the Perry Communication days, still serves as a sounding board for many of my ideas, and offers encouragement when needed most. His input is greatly appreciated. John has received national recognition as editor of the Georgia Elks quarterly newspaper for many years.

Others who have contributed through the years include: **Don Kite**, friend and former customer, who was editor of the discontinued Parts Pups humor publication. Don still toils daily at Genuine Parts Company headquarters; **Tom Cooper**, a former colleague at Perry, who serves as historian of the Atlanta Rotary Club. He is also an expert photographer; and, **Denver Gray**, a friend I gave some help to by compiling and editing his two books. His latest, recounting the experiences of Pearl Harbor survivors, including his own, is now ready for publication.

Two relatively new to my list are **Dr. William Suttles** and **Dan Berry**. Bill, as I call him, is the pastor emeritus of a small Baptist Church at Haralson Ga., where he served for 50 years. He also served for two decades as provost and executive vice president of Georgia State University, and was interim president for awhile. Dan, an inveterate reader of books, retired as advertising director of Georgia Marble Company. Dan absorbs a couple of books each day. He critiqued some of my writing and gave very helpful advice.

Other regular cronies at Mary Mac's Tea Room who have likewise aided me are: **Neil Thomas**, inventor of the super water-proofer DAMTITE; **Milton Vincent**, world champion horseshoe pitcher, **Jim Griffith**, former Ford Motor Company magnate; and **Julius Efron**, highly successful entrepreneur, who jokingly relates from his experiences, "how to run a million dollars into a shoestring." (Unfortunately, Julius passed away about a year ago. He is greatly missed by all of us.)

Most of these I mention appear, without being identified, in a photograph with me printed elsewhere in this book.

CONTENTS

Acknowledgments 5
Preface 9
A Clarification: How I AIM to Inspire and Motivate You 11
Chapters
One   Exploring My Bolton Roots 13
Two   Expanding My Horizons 25
Three   High School, Puberty... and More 29
Four   College Daze 35
Five   Beginning My Quest for a Pulitzer Prize 47
Six   Growing Up Too Fast, Too Soon 75
Seven   Censoring — Somebody Had To Do It 81
Eight   Looking Up "Down Under" 89
Nine   The Haugland Story 93
Ten   A Welcome Interlude of Home-Leave 103
Eleven   An Evening With Irving Berlin 109
Twelve   Drama in Manila 117
Thirteen   Borneo Invasion 121
Fourteen   Final Destination: Tokyo 127
Fifteen   General MacArthur at Atsugi 131
Sixteen   Hero and Traitor at Yokohama 135
Seventeen   Tokyo Excursion 139
Eighteen   Japanese Impressions 145
Nineteen   General MacArthur as I Knew Him 149
Twenty   The Surrender Ceremony 153
Twenty-One   Return to Marietta and Civilian Life 165
Twenty-Two   Transition Time: Hopping From
                 Little Pond to Big Pond 177
Twenty-Three   What Inspired and Motivated Me
                 to Live Past 87 193
Twenty-Four   Reflections on Life by an Octogenarian 197
Twenty-Five   Margaret Mitchell, GWTW... and Me 199
Twenty- Six   'Writing for the Lust of It' 201
About the Author 205

PREFACE

This book represents a non-living legacy, one of my few remaining ones. That's not to say it's dead in any sense. To the contrary, this writing has become the living embodiment of me - truly reflecting my aspirations and my achievements.

Critics - whether family, friends, or others - will determine if this legacy deserves plaudits or brickbats. There will be mixed reviews, I'm sure, whether I'm around to receive them or not.

The book makes a strong statement touting success. It parades my life as a worthy example, despite some failures. This is not said boastfully, but as a matter of fact.

Counselling for achieving this: "The only way to become a wise man is to outlive your contemporaries - and keep your mouth shut."

An observation: "When you reach 80, each year there's not a tombstone, is a milestone."

At my age, there are not many more brass rings to grasp on life's tenuous merry-go-round. On that sombre note, I end this preface while still expressing the hope that my writing will provide some measure of inspiration, as well as enjoyment.

A Clarification

HOW I <u>AIM</u> TO INSPIRE AND MOTIVATE YOU

<u>AIM</u> readily springs to mind as an acronym for "<u>A</u>spiring to <u>In</u>spire and <u>M</u>otivate." The word "aim" connotes purpose, and with a strong enough purpose, you can achieve anything within reason. It's axiomatic that the higher you aim, the more inspired and motivated you must become.

Throughout this book, there are many passages which, taken in the proper context, should inspire and motivate the reader.

In discussing the slant of the material with Wallace Cato, my good friend (at least until now) and (sometime) mentor, he advised that inspirational and motivational were the only type of personal experience writing the book publisher he represents would consider.

So <u>A</u>spiring to do just that has been my <u>A</u>im.

Further to the point, here's how I responded, in part, in an e-mail to Wally:

> ... I am attempting to be more inspirational and motivational. I believe much of my writing already qualifies in this respect. If you will read carefully, there are many references to what inspired and motivated me. Some of it is subtle, but I believe that is better than being so blatantly obvious...

> Then, too, I believe my entire life - my successes and accomplishments, despite sometimes seemingly overwhelming odds - will be generally inspirational and motivational. This should be said for clarification, even at the risk of being egocentric.

Exploring My Bolton Roots

This book's title, "Living By the Seat of My Pants!," puts a humorous twist on an old expression I first heard while growing up on the outskirts of Atlanta. Humor remains the mainstay of my life, helping to withstand the trials and tribulations experienced during my 87-year existence. Without the balm of humor, my survival would have been in jeopardy and my sanity in question at several critical stages.

Two catastrophic events defined my early life - the Great Depression and World War II. Yet, I derived lasting benefits from both that have helped me achieve whatever success I have had. I believe it's called serendipity, when good results accidentally.

The depression taught me many lessons about thrifty living and gave me an appreciation of my abundant blessings, including those that resulted only from a fortunate God-given inheritance of good genes.

The war changed and enhanced my life. Although the experiences were at times daunting and demanding, the educational value was inestimable. I realize that now more than I did at the time.

I was born on February 14, 1915, in Bolton, Georgia, a small community in the northern suburbs of Atlanta. My mother's brother, Dr. Paul McDonald, attended the delivery. A general practitioner, he treated the ills of most of the community. As was customary, the birth occurred at our home, a small, shot-gun frame house on Bolton Road.

When I was six weeks old, my family moved to a more spacious house on the same road only a quarter of a mile away. Still no indoor plumbing. For us, it was a room and a path. Believe me, it got cold going to the outhouse in that sometimes frigid weather. Our only water supply, a deep well, required each bucketfull to be cranked up on a rope coiled around a windlass. On

Saturday nights, a large amount of water had to be drawn for our weekly baths - whether we needed one or not. Of course, we had no central heat. Fireplaces in the bedrooms and a coal-burning kitchen stove had to suffice. We lived in this house until I was 10 years old when my father became affluent enough to build a new brick house just a hundred yards farther up the road.

The author at an early age, with his mother,
Annie Lee McDonald Hughes.

Several years before we moved, tragedy stuck our family. It affected all of us, but especially my parents. In 1922, another son, Miles Jr., had been born. A beautiful, happy child with deep dimples in both cheeks, he contracted a not uncommon child's disease of that day known as mastoiditis. After a brief period of suffering he passed away at the age of five months. Mother was devastated and I don't believe she ever fully recovered. Ironically, that type of severe ear infection can now be treated and cured.

I was seven years old at the time and attempted to console my mother as best I could. Our entire family, including my older siblings - sister, Hortense, age 14, and my brother, Donald, 12 - grieved for months, along with mother and daddy.

The new house was a vast improvement over the old. Built of brick, with four bedrooms, it featured that marvelous invention called indoor plumbing, even though there was only one bathroom which, it soon became evident, was a big mistake. Again, the only heat came from fireplaces. In the kitchen was one of the first electric stoves in Bolton, and I was duly proud of that and loved to show it off to my friends. The trade name imprinted on the front of the stove was "Hotpoint Hughes," and I told everyone that the appliance had been specially made for us.

Our home was situated just a few hops and skips from the heart of Bolton. This was at the intersection of Bolton Road and Highway 41, known as the Marietta highway. At one corner of the intersection stood my father's general grocery store, the only one in Bolton.

As owner and operator of that store, my father was known by everybody - and everybody knew him to be an honest, God-loving man who lived by the Golden Rule. He was known to be kind-hearted, extending credit to many of the needy who were not credit-worthy. He visited the sick regularly, including those of black families. I never heard anyone speak ill of my father. He had no enemies, to my knowledge. For awhile, he served as postmaster. The post office was in a corner section of the store. All mail was delivered to him from the train depot in sacks, which he sorted out and placed in private boxes for those who rented one. Other mail he filed alphabetically for general delivery and handed out to those who asked for their mail. He also wrote money orders and carried out the other duties of a postmaster.

At that time, I was the envy of my schoolmates. I could walk into the store and reach behind the counter for a handful of delicious candy, without charge. My father stopped this practice after awhile.

Me, at age eight.

My mother's brother, Dr. Paul, as he was called by family members, was noted for his "pink" medicine, a concoction tinged by that color that he mixed himself and dispensed seemingly to all patients, whether for a sore throat or for the whooping cough. Only he knew what the ingredients were. But it usually cured their ailments and his patients revered him, coming from miles away for treatment.

Being a generous person, he never charged us for his services because of the family connection. I remember on one occasion he sat up half the night attending my mother who was suffering from a serious heart condition. She recovered, I am convinced, due to his devotion to her and his medical skills. Still, no bill for his services. And that certainly fit the Hughes' budget at that time, which was in the midst of the depression.

As the official physician of Fulton County, Dr. Paul was required to visit the various prison camps and treat the inmates. He allowed me to accompany him on one of these visits, while I was still a small boy. These were the convicts who worked on the county's roads from dawn to dusk. I still recollect the painful experience of seeing first-hand the living conditions at this camp. Prisoners were penned together like animals, with some suffering from various stages of disease, one even with syphilis, a guard told me. Dr. Paul administered to them as best he could with the most advanced medical technology of the day, but no amount of "pink" medicine could have cured all of their ailments.

Dr. Paul was also versatile. I recall he played a cornet solo at several church services I attended. He also taught the men's bible class for many years.

Bolton was unincorporated, but several prominent families comprised the civic, social and religious hierarchy of the town.

Besides the various McDonald families (including the kinfolks of my mother and Dr. Paul), others included the Moores, the Wilsons, the Warrens, the Chambers, the Daniels, and the Gramblings.

Of these, the three Moore families stood out. One family, headed by long-time Fulton County Superior Court Judge Virlyn B. Moore Sr., was looked upon as the leader in any civic or religious endeavor and he wielded more clout and influence than anyone in the community.

His son, Virlyn Jr., was my boyhood idol. He exemplified all of the qualities I admired most and was my role model. He excelled in two major sports, baseball and basketball. I was privileged to practice with him a few times in those sports.

Members of the Moore family also engaged in other sports. I remember on one occasion his father joined us in a practice session of football. I had a new leather helmet and was eager to check out its effectiveness in protecting my skull. The judge was a rather portly gentleman (even though he had been an outstanding football player on the University of Georgia team just before the turn of the century), and I lined up opposite him. As the ball was snapped, I lunged forward and butted him with my new helmet in his ample stomach. He grunted and fell forward to the ground with his eyes closed. I was quite relieved when he revived and sat up. I wore that helmet for several years afterwards in neighborhood play, but never butted anyone in the midsection again.

Virlyn Jr. had two younger brothers, James and Bobby, and they were good athletes, also, but they never came close to their older brother's playing ability. In fact, Virlyn - a catcher - was offered a reportedly healthy contract to play baseball with the Atlanta Crackers, as well as some big league teams, which he turned down. Then, too, the famed Celtics basketball team tried to sign him after he scored so well playing against them in an exhibition game. He also refused this offer, obviously preferring to begin his legal practice, after which he entered the banking business. Of course, he was eminently successful, and served for many years as head of the Trust Department of Fulton National

Bank. Later, he became president of the Woodrow Wilson Law School.

Incidentally, I heard recently that Virlyn, always a Bolton booster, has written a history of the town. I certainly plan to buy, beg or borrow a copy and read it.

Virlyn's brother, James, was nearer my age and became one of my closest friends while growing up. I spent a number of nights at the Moore home as the guest of James and came to know all of the family well. Occasionally, he would stay at my home overnight, but I enjoyed being at his place more because the food was better and more plentiful. The Moores had two ponies, Buttons and Brownie, which James and I rode together with much pleasure. For me, it was the nearest thing to having a pony of my own - every boy's dream. James rode fast and recklessly at times, and I admired his "ponymanship," if I may coin such a word.

Another prominent Moore family had at its head Thomas Walter Moore, older brother of the judge. Walter held a high executive position with the General Electric Corporation, being in charge of its lighting division throughout Georgia, as I recall.

This is not a "kiss and tell" type of book, but Walter Moore's daughter, Martha, was the first girl I dated and the first girl I kissed. This occurred about the tender age of 12 and resulted in no earth-shattering repercussions. The date was a chaperoned ride to a neighbor's house for a prom party, an innocent type of affair popular in those days. The kiss, a hasty peck, was delivered and received a few days later, with little aplomb, while standing on a wooden bridge over a railroad track with both of us wearing roller skates. What a relief to get this confession off my conscience!

Martha and I remained friends after that and we attended the same high school in Atlanta, but we never dated again. I do remember in our senior play, she was my romantic interest, and I sang her a love song. By then, we both had other real life romantic interests, I'm sure.

Other boyhood friends of mine included Pierce McDonald, Leon Wilson, and J.O. Chambers. Pierce, the second oldest son of Dr. Paul, was the unacknowledged leader of our group which we called "The Fearful Four." This name, we thought, would strike terror in the minds of our contemporaries. However, this was not the forerunner of youth gangs as they exist today. We merely were drawn together by our mutual interests, and never engaged in real devilment of any kind. Pierce went on to become a successful dentist, but, tragically, he and his wife, Adelaide, died in the Orly-Paris plane crash on June 3, 1962, which took the lives of so many prominent Atlantans.

Seventh grade class of Bolton School pictured in 1927 with Principal Mrs. Vera Wilson in back row at right. I'm in the middle row at extreme left. Other members of the "Fearful Four" - J.O. Chambers, Pierce McDonald, Leon Wilson - are to the right of me (excluding the unidentifiable girl).

Leon, a next door neighbor for 20 years or so, was the son of Mrs. Vera Wilson, the highly esteemed principal of Bolton Grammar School. J.O. Chambers lived near the church we all attended and his father, Gus, sang bass in the choir in which my father was a tenor.

Like most young boys, I was very active and took more than my share of chances. Without seeming overly dramatic, it's a near-miracle I lived to adulthood. I had many close calls - from recklessly roller skating on roadways in heavy traffic to diving into shallow pools of water from considerable heights. Once my head landed on a tree root after being thrown from a playground swing at school and I received a deep gash in my skull. I haven't been the same since. Guess I was a daredevil and showoff.

One chilling memory stands out above all others. Today, I have as a reminder a jagged, five-inch scar on the outer thigh of my left leg. It happened one balmy summer day while Leon and Pierce and I were swimming, as customary, au naturel, in the muddy waters of the Chattahoochee River near Bolton.

At that point a steel cable stretched across the swift-flowing river to a small man-made island, which we reached with the aid of the cable. While exploring the island, I slipped and fell on the head of a 20-penny nail sticking up about an inch from a heavy wet board. The result: I was lying on my left side with the nail deeply impaled in my outer thigh.

With all the strength and will I could muster, I was forced to rise and lift myself from the board and off the nail head. As I did so, I remember looking down and seeing flesh hanging out from both sides of the gaping wound. Oh, yes, the nail was rusty.

Then came the problem of how to negotiate the river. With the aid of Leon and Pierce, and using the cable as best I could, I was able to cross. Somehow we got dressed and walked the couple hundred yards to the City of Atlanta water pumping station where help was provided in the form of a car and driver to take me to a doctor. By then the wound was bleeding profusely and I remember feeling faint.

A trip to Dr. Paul's home-office proved futile as he was not in. So we drove a few miles west to the Riverside community where fortunately a Dr. Redd was available to care for me. Of course, he washed the wound with the best antiseptic medicine of the day, but that was before antibiotics. He then sewed up the wound, taking several stitches.

Today, I feel fortunate to have survived the ordeal that could have ended in real tragedy. The scar remains as testimony to my sometimes reckless boyhood.

About a quarter of a mile south of the main intersection at Bolton was the grammar school where Mrs. Wilson presided with quiet authority. Stern but fair, she earned the respect of everyone. My teacher in the second grade was Aunt Mayme McDonald, wife of Homer, my mother's brother. At the end of the school year, she decreed that in view of my advanced state of learning, I should be allowed to skip the third grade and enter the fourth grade the following school year. This was done with Mrs. Wilson's concurrence.

Thereafter, I was in a grade with older peers, and I don't think I ever quite overcame the effects of skipping that grade - both socially and scholastically.

One incident in school resulted in my receiving a paddling, which I richly deserved; nevertheless, it was demeaning and caused me much mental anguish.

My fifth grade home room teacher was a comely young lady in her late teens named Willa Mae Carmichael. My brother, Donald, although younger than she, called and attempted to date her. I knew he didn't succeed, but just the fact that he called her made me feel like she was part of the family.

It was in that euphoric - but dumb - state of mind that I called out as she walked ahead of me one day on the road away from the schoolhouse: "Goodbye, Willa Mae." My childish reasoning was that she might not think I was addressing her, since there could possibly be another person by that name in the vicinity.

She knew I was referring to her, of course, and early the next morning I was called into the principal's office, where Miss Carmichael administered the paddling on my backside. The blows weren't hard. They mostly stung my pride.

There's more to tell about Miss Carmichael. She lived with her family across the Chattahoochee River from Bolton, on Highway 41, in Cobb County. Her father was a prosperous farm supplies merchant with an excellent reputation. His home and business were at Carmichael Stop, a station on the electric rail line between Atlanta and Marietta.

A couple of years after the paddling incident, we received word at school one day that Jimmy Carmichael, younger brother of Willa Mae, had been struck by an automobile and seriously injured while walking under the rail track near where the road ran too. A car lost control, pinning him against a wall. It happened near the high school he attended.

We were stunned by the news. Jimmy was known as one of the brightest and most promising young men in our area. His legs were badly mangled. Finally he began a slow recovery, but he never walked again without the aid of crutches or a cane.

During Jimmy's protracted convalescence, it was generally known that his sister, Willa Mae, contributed greatly to his recovery, especially to his mental and emotional well-being. Using her teaching skills, she patiently tutored him. Under her guidance he became very proficient at public speaking, which stood him in good stead in his later professional life, both as a lawyer and as a politician. In fact, he became widely recognized as one of the most accomplished speakers in Georgia politics, serving several terms in the Georgia General Assembly as Speaker of the House of Representatives.

One night in 1938, I sat at the Marietta Country Club with Jimmy Carmichael and other friends listening to the state election returns on the radio. In the gubernatorial race, Jimmy was a strong contender opposing the former governor, Eugene Talmadge, and many thought the Cobb Countian would defeat him. And Jimmy would have if it had not been for the outmoded county unit system of voting, which gave more weight to votes in the smaller counties that those in larger ones.

As we listened that night, Jimmy was leading in the popular vote by a substantial margin, but when the smaller counties reported their voting results, Jimmy lost out. He still received a majority of the popular vote, which was an outstanding accomplishment in view of Talmadge's long entrenchment in Georgia politics.

Willa Mae married Earl Williams, owner and operator of a drug store on the city square in Marietta. Earl and I, as well as Jimmy Carmichael, were members of the Marietta Kiwanis Club. Naturally, in the few casual social contacts I had with Willa Mae, neither of us mentioned the paddling incident. And, of course, I always addressed her as Mrs. Williams, not Willa Mae, even though I called Earl by his first name.

By this time, Jimmy was married to my first cousin, Frances McDonald, daughter of Homer and Mayme McDonald, which made me feel even closer to the Carmichaels. You will read much more about my life and newspaper career in Marietta in later segments of this writing, if you are still with me.

Throughout my boyhood, Collins Memorial Methodist Church maintained its role as the heart and soul of Bolton. Constructed in the traditional architectural style of the period and situated about half a mile west of the center of town, the church was an inspiring old edifice which still exists. It was here we gathered, good weather or bad, every Sunday for worship services, as well as to socialize.

For years, Mrs. "Robb" Moore, wife of the judge, was the choir director. Among the choir members at various times were my sister, my daddy, and me. My sister sang an occasional solo, and after the untimely death of Mrs. Moore, succeeded her as director. Virlyn Jr. remained in the group. He had quite a good bass voice.

At different times, both Virlyn Jr. and Sr., taught Sunday School classes which I attended. They were great teachers and I looked forward to hearing their common sense, home-spun reflections on life and religion. The judge was especially good at this, sometimes almost profound. Once Virlyn Jr. told my mother that judging from my quick responses in class, I showed some aptitude as a Bible student. Of course, that raised my somewhat fragile ego at least one notch.

At homecoming each summer, church members gathered outdoors for a spread of food so plentiful and delicious as to make sinful gluttons of us all. This was the time when members of the Collins Memorial congregation met in Christian fellowship. We all enjoyed the occasion each year. Even former members who had moved away returned when they were able.

Both my grandfather, Alfred Turner McDonald, and his twin brother, Allen Pierce McDonald, were charter members of the church and attended services regularly. Interestingly, the brothers married sisters in ceremonies two years apart on Christmas Eve in Campbell County. Both men were carpenters and lived with their families the latter stages of their lives on Bolton Road.

For many years, the McDonalds far outnumbered any other family in Bolton. At one time, there were eight McDonald families in residence, all living within the radius of one mile. This resulted in a closeness that would be rare among families today. Many Sundays, after church, a sumptuous noonday meal would be served at grandmother's house, with the women bringing the food. Of course, we children would eat at the "second table," but we never left hungry.

Collins Memorial Methodist Church on Bolton Road.

EXPANDING MY HORIZONS

L eaving the confines of Bolton in the summer of 1925, my horizons were greatly expanded by a trip to North Carolina and New York. What an adventure for a 10-year-old!

I was accompanied on the train trip to Lewiston, North Carolina, by my father's nephew, Ed Broughton Hoggard, a Bolton resident, who was returning for a visit to his old home town.

My father was born and raised in Lewiston, a small rural community situated in the flat country of eastern North Carolina. He and my mother married and lived there for several years before moving to Georgia, and my sister and brother were born in the

Tar Heel state. It was interesting to see my father's old homeplace and meet his kinfolks.

After about a week, Ed Broughton and I boarded a train for Norfolk, then another for New York City. We were met in New York by my namesake Edmund W. Corrie, whom I was to visit for the next seven days, and Ed Broughton left to return to Atlanta as planned. That night we stayed at the Commodore Hotel, which was sheer luxury. I was overwhelmed by its grandeur and opulence, and Mr. Corrie seemed pleased by my reaction. Next morning after a delightful breakfast, we left by train for Albany, where Mr. Corrie was cashier of a branch of the New York State Bank.

Edmund W. Corrie,
my namesake.

By way of explanation, my father had met Mr. Corrie when the New Yorker was traveling by bicycle through North Carolina years before while on vacation. After their initial meeting, they became good friends and carried on a regular correspondence thereafter. Upon my birth, my parents decided to name me Edmund Corrie because of their friendship with him. Every Christmas, he sent me a two-and-a-half dollar gold piece as a present. How impressive to me that was.

That week in Albany was memorable, but somewhat bittersweet. Never having been away from home before, the strange environment soon palled on me and I became homesick.

Mr. and Mrs. Corrie had no children of their own and were not accustomed to catering to the whims of a 10-year-old. What a trial I must have been for them. Yet, they couldn't have been more considerate. Several times he took me with him to his office in the bank. He gave me a large number of coins - some rare and somewhat valuable - from the horde he had collected through the years as a teller. But, alas, some of them were counterfeit I learned to my disappointment when I tried to spend them back at home.

I remember the Corries tried every way to entertain me, including a visit to the State Capitol building. Once they took me to a movie titled "Coast of Folly" with Gloria Swanson in the lead. It was not a child's movie, but I thoroughly enjoyed it. How could anyone named Gloria not be glamorous? Many years later I learned she had been the mistress of multi-millionaire Joseph Kennedy, father of JFK. How very disillusioning - even now!

When my visit ended, Mr. Corrie escorted me back to New York City and put me on a train bound for Atlanta. I traveled alone, perhaps too young for such a trip, but I survived thanks to some good people I met in the Pullman and dining cars. One such person, a young man unable to walk without crutches, became my friend. When we reached the Terminal Station, I thought no one had come to meet me. I later learned by mother arrived on time with Cousin Charlie McDonald, but the train was ahead of schedule. Anyway, we missed each other.

I panicked a little at this turn of events. Next I reasoned that mother had expected the train to arrive at the Brookwood Station across town, where I had left from beginning the trip. So I persuaded my handicapped friend to go with me in a taxi to the Brookwood Station to find my mother. He did so graciously and paid the cab fare since it was near the place he was going anyway. Mother was not at Brookwood, so I did what I should have done before and called home, where mother by then had returned. How relieved we both were. Another cab brought me home.

What a grand reunion we had when I walked in the door. Tales of my travel experiences resounded on into the night, and were repeated for years afterwards to anyone who would listen.

HIGH SCHOOL, PUBERTY... AND MORE

I entered high school and reached puberty at about the same time. And, as unsophisticated as I was, being just 12 years old, I was ill prepared for either.

Of the two, high school provided the most trauma... and drama. The biggest problem was the travel required, since the school was situated across downtown Atlanta from Bolton, a distance of some eight miles. This meant getting up at daybreak and boarding a streetcar (as they were called then) with other sleepy-eyed riders for the daily trek to Atlanta. There we transferred to another trolley which took us to Fulton High School on Washington Street, just west of the State Capitol Building.

The trip took more than an hour. Thus, we spent two hours each day in travel.

High School studies proved more difficult for me. I attribute this partially to my skipping the third grade in grammar school, which must have left a gap in my basic educational background. This was true especially in math, which I never had much aptitude for anyway. I remember it was in the third grade that students were introduced to fractions; I still have trouble with fractions today.

Contributing to my poor scholastic showing was my newly found interest in girls. My grades went down in direct proportion to the degree of my thinking about the members of the opposite sex.

I became acquainted, of course, with a number of students, boys and girls, although I was not very outgoing and did not make friends easily. This was partially due to my young age, as well as to an innate shyness which I attempted to conceal. My contact with girls was limited to an exchange of a few smiles and brief conversations. Later on in high school I began dating, but since my family had no automobile except for my sister's 1928

Model A-Ford, which she was reluctant to let me drive, this was curtailed by the lack of transportation. That, however, is another story...

One important aspect of my high school days was the military training I received through ROTC. It was compulsory to enroll in either the ROTC or physical education classes. Fortunately, I chose the former. I wore the baggy, dark brown wool uniform of that era with the wrap leggins. What a chore to get dressed, and how hot the uniform was in warm weather!

The program was basic, and what I learned served me well at the University of Georgia and later in the Army. Both emphasized the manual of arms, and I became adept at handling the old World War I vintage Springfield rifle we used in drilling.

(In 1935, while a sophomore at Georgia, I won a medal for being the "Best Drilled Soldier" in ROTC manual-of-arms competition. I was elated when I won, and the news was reported in both the Athens and Atlanta newspapers. The president of the University, Dr. S.V. Sanford, presented the medal to me in person during a Honors Day program, with a goodly number in attendance. I remember he said as he made the presentation, "I wish I had been the best in something." I still have the medal tucked away among my scattered mementoes.)

Although I was never really proficient in many athletic endeavors, sports played a big part in my adolescent years. The sport I enjoyed the most was tennis.

One of my fondest memories remains the annual tennis tournament sponsored by Collins Memorial Church, played on the three courts behind the church. About 25 or 30 men entered each year and the competition was keen. Fortunately, I was playing my best at that time and won the event three straight years. This allowed me to keep the small trophy cup. I still have it. Another treasured keepsake.

But tennis had its downside for me. I overdid it. One summer I played 13 sets of singles in one day. That's a lot of tennis, and I ended up going to bed with heart pains. A doctor was called who diagnosed my condition as a heart murmur. He said I might outgrow it, and, apparently I did, because no other doctor has ever detected it, including a number of army doctors. Nevertheless, I was confined to bed for a couple of weeks and did not play tennis again for awhile.

While at Fulton High, I did earn a letter in tennis, playing in a number of matches with other schools. Also, one year I entered the city of Atlanta tennis tournament. But I didn't win a match, having drawn Malon Courts, the city champion in the first round.

Clipped from the Atlanta Journal. Caption refers to first round of city tennis tournament. I'm the skinny guy in center of photo. At extreme left is my cousin, Morris McDonald. Jeff Warren, a good friend also from Bolton, is second from right. None of us won our matches.

(In 1933, during my freshman year at Oglethorpe University, I advanced to the finals of the schoolwide tennis tournament, but a southpaw named Gene Ray from Acworth soundly defeated me. Just recently I read in the newspaper that Gene Ray, now in his eighties, had won some senior tournament in Atlanta.)

Basketball was my second best sport during adolescence, but an unfortunate accident derailed my dreams of becoming a star. During my sophomore year at Fulton High I went out for the basketball team. I had played in grammar school and practiced with members of Virlyn Moore's family, as mentioned in a previous segment. I was not tall and probably would have been rated as an average player.

At the first practice session I attended, at the Atlanta City Auditorium, I was being boosted up to untangle a net caught up in the goal hoop, when I began to fall. I grabbed for the hoop, but the goal, a portable type, tilted over, fell on me, and knocked me unconscious. An ambulance was called and I was taken to Grady Hospital. There I regained consciousness and it was determined I was not seriously injured. But that ended my aspirations for basketball stardom.

I'll never forget how relieved the coach, E.P. McIlwain, was after my recovery. He happened to be my home room teacher and expressed his relief to the class the next day.

In those early days, golf was considered a rich man's sport because of the expensive equipment required and the amount of time it took to play a round. None of my friends had clubs or attempted to play. My brother Donald made a half-hearted attempt using homemade clubs and old balls in a nearby cow pasture, but he was never very successful. I had little interest.

(Later, during my adulthood, golf would become the main recreational outlet throughout my business career and it played a large role in my social life. More about golf later.)

Football was another sport I attempted to engage in without much success. Because of my small size and lack of weight, I never became a candidate for a school team. However, I did learn to pass fairly well and enjoyed other aspects of the game.

One season we organized a neighborhood team and called ourselves the "Skull Busters." We played other neighborhood teams and succeeded in winning a number of games.

Then, Leo Carlton, the local grocer, arranged a game for us with the inmates of the Federal Penitentiary on Confederate Avenue in Atlanta. This was rather scary. We were a diverse, hodge-podge group without any real football experience. We also lacked the proper uniform equipment. The inmates practiced daily, we heard, and were provided with the best in equipment. While dressing for the game, I remember, we picked up and used some of their castoff helmets, shoulder pads and the like.

While warming up before the game, one of the guards (they served as officials) said to me, pointing to one of the two men playing tennis on a court near the football field: "He is Al Capone," (an infamous former Chicago gangster, who I had forgotten was in the Atlanta Pen). When we started playing, they came over and sat in the viewing stands and watched the entire game. The guard explained that the man with Capone was one of his bodyguards who always accompanied him to prevent him from being killed by fellow inmates.

Before the game started, as captain of our team, I met with their captain for the coin toss made by a guard-official. I've forgotten who won the toss, but I do remember the game was rough and rugged. They had some ex-college players who were in good physical condition. We had no set plays and did not call signals. As quarterback, I would take charge of the huddle and describe the upcoming play, whether a run with a designated ball carrier, or a pass to a particular receiver.

This didn't work well, for we failed to score and lost the game 8 to 0. They scored a touchdown and then a safety by catching me behind our goal line while attempting to pass. Still, considering the odds against us, we gave a pretty good accounting of ourselves.

While walking down the bleak, gloomy corridors leaving the prison, we passed through a series of heavy metal doors, which were unlocked to let us pass. At each door stood a steely-eyed guard who peered intently into our faces to make sure none of us was an inmate attempting to gain his freedom. The entire experience, if nothing else, would serve as a deterrent to my committing a crime carrying a federal prison sentence.

COLLEGE DAZE

In the first segment of these writings, I stated that the Great Depression was one of the two catastrophic events that defined my early life, the other being World War II.

Beginning with the stock market crash in 1929, the depression lingered for several years and adversely affected my plans for entering the University of Georgia immediately after finishing high school. I, as well as my parents, were determined that I get a college education. My sister, Hortense, had graduated from LaGrange College and was now teaching at Bolton Grammar School. My brother, Donald, was a junior at Georgia. Luckily, he needed no financial assistance from the family as he earned enough money selling magazines during the summer months to pay all of his college expenses. He even owned an automobile.

At this time, in 1933, my father was doing reasonably well in the insurance business in Atlanta, but we all felt some of the financial pinch that affected most everyone in the U.S. So it was decided that I should commute to Oglethorpe University here in Atlanta rather than enroll at Georgia with the expense of living in Athens.

It was arranged that I would ride to and from Oglethorpe, a distance of some eight miles, with Marie Mauldin, member of a Bolton family who was a senior at the school. Another passenger in the car was my first cousin, Lois McDonald, daughter of my uncle, Dr. Paul, who taught at E. Rivers School, and was dropped off and picked up there.

The plan was for me to attend Oglethorpe for one year and then transfer to Georgia to complete my education.

Except for math, courses at Oglethorpe were easy for me and I made respectable grades. I even made 100 one semester in an English course. But that was offset by my flunking a course in trigonometry. I still contend this weakness in math probably resulted from my skipping the third grade in grammar school. Or, maybe I'm just naturally dumb when it comes to math.

Oglethorpe was a social school (some said too much so) and I came to know some very likeable people there. Even though I had no thought then of studying journalism, it was there I received my first taste of news reporting. In an English class assignment, we were asked to write a news story about some happening on the campus. I chose to write about a couple of football players posing in the nude as models for an art class. To me, this was scandalous, earth-shaking news. I remember other class members laughed when I read my hot news story aloud as we were required to do.

At the end of the school year, the economy was still in the doldrums and my parents decided I should sell magazines as Donald did to help pay for my college education. Accordingly, my brother arranged an interview for me with his boss, a Mr. Withrow, in Atlanta. I was hired, largely, I suspect, because of Donald's influence.

Shortly thereafter, I set out for Florida traveling by automobile in a crew of four, including myself, to sell subscriptions to Good Housekeeping and Cosmopolitan magazines to unsuspecting housewives of the Sunshine State, or anyone else who would buy one. It turned out to be one of the most traumatic experiences of my entire life, including up to the present time. Our crew chief, a rotund individual called Smitty, was tough and demanding, which I realize now he needed to be in order to be successful. We crew members were verbally abused when we failed to make sales on which he received an override commission. This was in the midst of the depression and housewives had little discretionary money for magazines, or anything else.

It should be explained that Donald had his own crew and traveled throughout Alabama. Stories were legendary about how successful he had been for three years. Other salesmen told how he would ring a door bell and when the housewife appeared, he would smile and make some inane remark, usually posed in the form of a question, to get her attention and gain her goodwill, and then proceed to charm her into buying the subscription. Usually, she would invite him into the house. He made between $2,000 and $3,000 each summer. That was a lot of money in those days.

Whatever was required to be successful, I didn't have, and I soon realized it. As I remember, I didn't sell more than two or three subscriptions during the three weeks I "worked." After several days of making calls and being repeatedly turned down, I became distraught. Having only limited expense money, I ate mostly cheap, unwholesome foods and suffered for it physically. Finally, after living for two days on milk shakes only, I wired my father for money to return home on. He responded with a minimum amount and I hitchhiked back home to Bolton, feeling utterly defeated. Yet my mother, who was concerned about my weight loss, greeted me warmly.

At a family council, it was decided that I should remain out of college for a year and work at whatever type of employment I could find. This worried me because I knew that once a person dropped out of school and began working, he seldom returned to complete his education. But, fortunately, I would prove to be one of the exceptions. That next year was not a total waste, although I did miss the discipline of studying and attending class. By then I was becoming a more mature person in my thinking, having benefited from my failure as a magazines salesman. This helped strengthen my resolve to be a success in other endeavors, whether they involved direct selling or not.

Almost immediately, through a stroke of good fortune, I was hired as the night attendant at the automobile service station in the heart of Bolton. This meant working from 7 p.m. to 7 a.m., pumping gasoline, checking oil levels and tire pressures and carrying out other duties the job required. This was long before the automatic pump, and gas had to be hand pumped up into a 10-gallon glass container sitting atop the pump. the number of gallons dispensed into the car was measured by a gauge of numbers displayed through the glass container.

I was the only night attendant, of course, and I was required to keep records of all sales and make an accounting each morning when I was relieved of duty by the owner. This was good training and taught me some of the basics of business. One drawback:

I consumed more soft drinks and snack foods than I should have since they were so readily available.

After a month or so, the owner decided the night business was not profitable enough to justify staying open, so my job came to an end. The pay was only a dollar or two a night (I forget how much), but it was a good learning experience and kept me from spending money I did not have.

Second row, extreme left is Benteen McDonald, my first cousin.

It was then that I, inadvertently, turned to some non-paying community services involving Bolton Grammar School. By this time, the school had moved from Bolton Road into a handsome new brick edifice about a mile southeast in another neighborhood. My next door neighbor, Mrs. Vera Wilson, who was still principal, requested that I take over the job of coaching both the boys' and girls' basketball teams. I accepted the challenge and never regretted it since it turned out to be rewarding in every sense. I derived great pleasure from seeing the young students learn teamwork and develop into capable basket shooters and ball handlers. I do not take full credit for their success, for they were talented and determined, but both teams - the boy's and the girls' - won their respective championships, defeating all other grammar school teams in Fulton County in a tournament at the end of the season.

I spent the remainder of that school year and summer mostly engaging in two other sports - tennis and football. Tennis, my favorite, I played as often as I could. As for football, it was during this period that I played with the "Skull Busters" against the Atlanta Federal Penitentiary inmates, described in the preceding segment.

Enrolling at Georgia that fall of 1934 was the realization of a long-cherished dream. Brother Donald had graduated the year before, and he accompanied me to Athens to register. I was relieved that they accepted all of my credits from Oglethorpe. Thus, I was a full-fledged sophomore.

One of the family's conditions for my attending Georgia was that I work part-time to help reduce the financial burden on my father. I was able to obtain a job under the National Youth Administration program paying 30 cents an hour. So I worked two hours each weekday for just 60 cents. But, a Coke cost a nickel, as I remember, and a loaf of bread a dime.

I was interviewed for the job by Mrs. Mary Bondurant, personnel director, who assigned me to the main administrative office of the University. The work was easy, mostly clerical, and I breezed through it.

(Looking ahead: Mrs. Bondurant became my mentor, advising and helping me, and two years later, for a journalism assignment, I interviewed her and wrote a several-page article for the "Georgia Arch" magazine titled "Odd Jobs.")

Before leaving Athens, Donald took me to his old fraternity house on Lumpkin Street and introduced me to his Sigma Nu brothers. They were friendly and cordial, and invited me to become a pledge, which I did. However, I didn't join later that year, as I had expected to do, not only because I didn't have the $75 initiation fee, but also because regulations would not permit NYA beneficiaries to join a fraternity requiring dues payments. I remained a pledge, however, and had my meals at the house during that year.

Front Row, L to R - Fames Curtis, Lee Parker, Wallace Jamison, Ben Anderson, John Bond, Gene Curry, Dan Morrell, Edmund Hughes.
Back Row, L to R - Henry Tart, Leon Wilson, Tom J. McRae, John Bell, and Charles Elrod.
Reprinted from Sigma News, annual bulletin of the Georgia chapter of Sigma Nu. I'm seated at right. Leon Wilson, my Bolton neighbor, is on back row.

It was at this stage that I began wearing glasses. For years, I had realized my vision was impaired and that I was missing too much in life by not seeing well. Tests confirmed this deficiency and I have worn glasses ever since. When I first put them on, I remember saying it was like "turning on the lights."

During the summer between my sophomore and junior years, I made the momentous (to me) decision to switch from Commerce to Journalism. I reached the decision after much consultation with family, and friends whose opinions I valued. The matter was clinched when it was learned that all of the commerce courses I had taken could be applied as electives towards a Bachelor of Arts in Journalism degree. Thus, I became a junior in the Henry W. Grady School of Journalism without having a single credit in Journalism. In retrospect, I have never regretted making the change.

Entering Journalism school marked a distinct turning point in my life and opened up exciting new vistas, including dreams of becoming a successful newspaperman. It had an immediate, stimulating import. Now I had a sense of purpose. I enjoyed the courses more, especially those involving news reporting. I liked the gathering of information and stringing facts together in a news story. And, one encouraging note: I discovered I had some aptitude for reporting and editing.

I admired and respected my professors, especially Dean John E. Drewry, who ranked high among journalism educators throughout the nation. I looked forward to his class lectures, which always sparkled with inimitable humor, and took copious notes. Dignified and proper, Dean Drewry always addressed his students as "Mr." and "Miss." (Years later, while working with an Atlanta printing firm, I knew I had arrived when Dean Drewry began a letter to me with, "Dear Edmund." Of course, I responded with a "Dear John" salutation.

The most popular course Dean Drewry taught was called "Magazines." This dealt with all aspects of then current magazines, including their founding and history, their editorial policies, and their failures and successes. His lectures were made more interesting by anecdotal sidelights.

He told how *Readers Digest* was started on a shoestring by the husband and wife team of DeWitt Wallace and Lila Acheson Wallace, who began reprinting articles from other publications after paying the original publishers an agreed upon amount. Then the Wallaces began contracting for reprint rights for all articles in many leading magazines, often voluntarily paying more that the publishers asked. Thus, they sewed up all the most desirable publishers, and eliminated any competition *Readers Digest* might have had.

We learned *Time* was founded by Henry Luce and a partner named Haddon, who originated the concept of a magazine presenting the weekly news in a concise, compelling style. Their success spawned other magazines by the same company, including *Life* and *Fortune*. Today, several news magazines pattern themselves after *Time*.

(In Manila, in 1945, I attended as a PR officer on General MacArthur's staff a small dinner party given by *Time* and *Life* war correspondents. About 10 or 12 people were invited to meet Mr. Henry Luce, who was visiting that war-torn city. I chatted with him briefly, and he came across as personable and down to earth.)

Other Journalism courses I took covered newspaper histories, including biographies of leading journalists, short story writing, and more practical matters such as touch typing and setting type by hand. One of the most useful things I learned was touch typing, which meant I could type without looking at the keyboard. This helped immensely in my newspaper work.

We learned reporting by doing just that - reporting. For one assignment, I attended Sunday morning services at the First Methodist Church in Athens and wrote a news story about the sermon. My byline story appeared on the front page of the *Athens Banner Herald* newspaper the next day. For this, I received no compensation, but the experience was invaluable.

I also wrote stories for the *Red and Black*, student newspaper, and the *Georgia Arch*, a quarterly magazine.

None of the stories I wrote for Short Story class had the distinction of being published, although I submitted several to various magazines. One of the rejection letters referred to my masterpiece as "amateurish," much to my chagrin. I recall that the title of that story was "Abductor Preferred." Small wonder it was turned down.

During my three years at Georgia, my most enjoyable and satisfying extracurricular activity was singing in the Glee Club. I had always been interested in music and singing, although I could not read a note, having turned down my sister's offer to teach me at an early age because of a stronger interest in athletics.

Nevertheless, I tried out for the club and was invited to join as a first tenor. I learned later first tenors were scarce because so few men had a high enough singing voice. That deflated me a little.

Genial Hugh Hodgson, the director, was dedicated and brought out the best tonal qualities in our youthful voices. He possessed a dramatic flair for directing that resulted in overflow crowds at most Glee Club concerts.

Each year during the spring quarter, the Glee Club made a week's tour to South Georgia, giving concerts at various colleges and other institutions. These, too, were well attended. Following a performance at a girls' college, we would meet and be entertained by (usually) attractive young female students. We traveled by chartered bus, and the three trips I took were highlights of my college career. One night after a concert in Savannah, a date was arranged for each of us, and we all partied at a night club in the old DeSoto Hotel. What memories!

Military training had a strong fascination for me and played a large role in my college life. As I wrote earlier, I won a medal my sophomore year in manual-of-arms competition with my fellow students. This fueled my interest and I made good grades in classroom studies.

One of the requirements for completing the advanced infantry military course was to attend a six-week summer training camp at Camp McClellan, Alabama. This was a rigorous program that tested us to the core, mentally and physically. Somehow I survived and ended up in vastly improved physical condition.

My junior year I achieved the rank of sergeant major and wore the distinctive chevrons of that grade on my sleeve. My senior year I became captain of "A" Company, and thus commanded the leading unit in drill and parade formations. I took especial pleasure in barking out commands during close order drill.

The military ball was a social highlight each year, and I escorted to the dance the girl I happened to be dating at the time.

The Scabbard and Blade was an honorary military society to which only a few seniors were invited to join each year. I was pleased to be included, although it was necessary to borrow the $100 initiation fee from a fraternal organization, the Knights of Columbus. For the record, I repaid this debt, with interest, within two years after graduation.

An even more significant honor came my way when I was elected to Sigma Delta Chi, prestigious national journalism fraternity. For more than 40 years I maintained this membership throughout my careers in journalism and printing, and I benefited from it greatly.

During the summer between my junior and senior years, I worked as an intern on the *Atlanta Constitution* and got a taste of big city newspapering; albeit, no remuneration. Assigned to work with T.K. Jones, the paper's top court reporter, the two of us covered the Atlanta Municipal Court, Grady Hospital, and the city jail. He did the reporting and writing. I listened and observed, and learned a great deal about reporting. Actually, T.K. usually did not write the stories, but called in the facts to a rewrite man at the *Constitution*.

Our working space was a small press room provided for newsmen of all three Atlanta newspapers, furnished with telephones and teletype machines. The reporter for the rival *Atlanta Georgian* happened to be William Randolph Hearst Jr., father of Patty Hearst, and I came to know him well. We called him Randy, never dreaming that one day he would figure so prominently in the Patty Hearst kidnapping incident.

One disturbing revelation came to light from my association with T.K. Jones. A top reporter on a major newspaper with ten years on the job, he was being paid only $30 a week. That gave me pause and influenced me in making a major career decision.

During the spring of my senior year, I received another large dose of on-the-job training when three fellow students and I were selected to spend a week in Lavonia and put out a complete edition of the weekly newspaper *Lavonia Times*, under the tutelage and discerning eye of publisher Rush Burton. We students - two men and two women - produced the entire editorial content, even to writing the editorials. The experience was not only enjoyable, but educational in the extreme. It also heightened my awareness to the desirability of small town newspaper work, and living, other than that of a big city environment, and influenced my decision to enter the weekly field, which I still believe was the right one for me.

Before leaving Lavonia, I talked to Mr. Burton about the possibility of working for him following graduation. However, we reached no agreement. When I returned to Athens, Dean Drewry informed me he had recommended me as a prospect for joining the staff of the *Cobb County Times* in Marietta. I was pleased and complimented. The *Times* was recognized as one of the best weeklies in Georgia, and Marietta was less than 20 miles from my home in Bolton.

But, first, after I graduated in June with the Reserve rank of second lieutenant, I had to fulfill a commitment to attend a two-week Officer Reserve Corps training camp at Camp McClellan. Completing this training meant that in three years I would automatically become eligible for advancement to first lieutenant in the Reserves. This would prove to be a wise decision for me.

Meanwhile, I wrote Editor Chess Abernathy and arranged an interview after the conclusion of my military duty. Two weeks later, he hired me for the munificent salary of $15 a week and with the title of managing editor. So I prepared to launch my journalistic career, with a few misgivings, but also with visions of a Pulitzer Prize dancing in my head.

Beginning My Quest for a Pulitzer Prize

M arietta, with a population of some 8,000 in 1937, was sometimes described as "lying in the shadow of historic Kennesaw Mountain." And metaphorically speaking, that's correct, even if not literally true.

While I was growing up in Bolton, Marietta was thought of as having an elitist society. Another adjective we heard was "clannish." But I found neither of these applicable.

Arriving in July 1937 to begin my duties as managing editor of the *Cobb County Times*, I was warmly welcomed by everyone. Being single and unattached may have been a contributing factor. Also, my job as a newspaper's representative provided entrees I may not have had otherwise.

Editor Chess Abernathy took me in tow and introduced me everywhere, including the newspaper office and printing plant, as well as around the City Square. Everyone I met was cordial and friendly. Chess and I had an immediate rapport, and this closeness would continue throughout our long working relationship. It should be noted that Chess was soon to be married to my first cousin, with whom I grew up, the former Martha McDonald, of Bolton.

It was then I also met Publisher Otis Brumby Sr., who would become a highly-respected father figure and my mentor.

But before getting fully involved in my work, I was forced to undergo a tonsillectomy that threatened to cut short my life. While being examined at ORC military camp, I was advised that my tonsils were badly infected and should be removed immediately.

After his own examination, Dr. Murl Hagood, general practitioner and surgeon, performed the operation at the old Marietta Hospital, just off the Square. Because of the advanced stage of the infection, following surgery, I was hemorrhaging. After much effort and several failures, the surgeon finally was able to resuture the incision. By then, I was weak and nauseated, and I barely survived. In fact, Dr. Hagood, who became a friend of mine, told me later that I came nearer to dying than any patient he had ever had who didn't do so.

After a few days in the hospital, during which I was visited by several kind-hearted people who were complete strangers to me, I was released. My recovery was hastened by my desire to get on with my career and begin my quest for a Pulitzer Prize.

(One of the aforementioned visitors during my hospital stay was an attractive young lady named Howard Perkinson, daughter of a prominent Marietta physician, who would return to Randolph Macon College as a student that fall. I remember she kissed me as she left. Later, Howard - her real name - became a good friend, and sometimes would ask me to date one of her roommates during home visit to Marietta. Recently, after a period of widowhood, Howard married deTreveille Lawrence, a former classmate of mine at Georgia, who also was cordial in welcoming me to Marietta in 1937. I forgot to mention Howard was the Beauty Queen at Randolph Macon her senior year, as her mother had been before her.)

After a brief time as a convalescent, I began the task of putting together a complete, full-size newspaper each week, which often required 14-hour work days. The job meant filling eight, twelve, or sixteen pages with acceptable local news. The emphasis was on "local," since the *Times*' reputation was solidly based on printing local news and not "boiler plate" syndicated filler material readily available for a fee.

The amount of advertising sold dictated the number of pages of a particular issue. Chess, our advertising manager, as well as editor, was responsible for all matters relating to advertising, including sales. He prepared a "dummy" for each page with the positioning of the advertisements indicated. I filled in the remaining space with news and editorial material. Chess occasionally wrote an editorial and a front page news story when he had the time.

We had a number of so-called "country correspondents" who each week mailed in, or brought by, the news of their districts in return for a free subscription to the newspaper. These reports, hand-written in simple, rural language, usually were about who had visited whom that week. I remember one phrase written repeatedly: So-and-so was the "spend the night guest" of so-and-so. I had to type each of these so that they would be readable by the linotype operator.

I wrote virtually all the editorials, but we had a couple of regular editorial columnists, including Editor Abernathy, whose weekly contribution titled "Now I Like That - " was widely read. But the most popular feature of the entire paper was Publisher Brumby's front-page column, "Jambalaya." Later, I would write an editorial page column titled "Hughes' Views." More about that will follow.

In writing editorials, I could "view with alarm" or "point with pride" at will, and with impunity. I had mostly free reign and tried to employ what common sense I possessed to follow the general editorial policies of the newspaper. These were unwritten, and there were few taboos or restrictions.

This does not mean we avoided controversy. Au contraire. We took definite stands on issues and welcomed a good fight. In 1938, a front page editorial Chess and I wrote together won first place for the "Most Fearless Editorial" appearing in any Georgia newspaper that year, including all dailies. The editorial, titled "You Yellow Rats," castigated the participants in a race riot at Smyrna. This was a major news story and my experiences in covering it, while "scooping" the big city reporters, will be described in full later.

Shortly after beginning my job, Betty Schilling, a columnist with the rival newspaper, the *Marietta Daily Journal*, wrote this: "Who is this person who calls himself Edmund Hughes?" by way of greeting me. I took no offense and soon became acquainted with Betty, who was the daughter of Marietta postmaster Walter Schilling, and later dated her a few times. A Phi Beta Kappa graduate of the University of Georgia, Betty married a West Point graduate and moved away from Marietta. Betty's sister, Madge, married Alec Tregone, editor of the rival daily newspaper, and he and I soon became friendly competitors.

The Owls vs. Marietta's Martins

In 1938, I put Marietta on the world map for a brief moment, and, incidentally, inflated my wallet as well as my ego. This happened when I sold a free-lance article I wrote to the *American Weekly*, a national newspaper supplement which claimed to have the "greatest circulation in the world." The article, titled "The Owls vs. Marietta's Martins," described the city's battle to drive away the hordes of pesky migratory birds that infested the city square each year. In correspondence with a representative of the *American Weekly*, I was offered $65, including photographs, for the article. In negotiating mode, I asked for and received $85.

The article, complete with photographs, some of which I took, made a big splash on a full right-hand page and spilled over to another page. Of course, I was not given a byline and much of it was rewritten. but the money - a goodly sum for those days - was gratefully received and put to good use.

The article recounted how the martins became such a nuisance that the city council voted funds to fight them. Several methods were tried to speed the departure of the annoying guests. The fire department squirted water up the trees with little effect. Shiny pieces of tin hung on strings to turn and flash in the wind was tried with the same result. Roman candles were shot into the trees, but not a single bird left town.

In this emergency, Councilman Frank Wellons was named generalissimo of the martin war with a modest appropriation for a "war chest."

In studying the matter, Frank learned that owls were natural enemies of martins and might prove to be the nemesis he sought. So he advertised for them - hoot owls, screech owls, great horned owls - any old kind of bird with a preference for extra size and visibility.

Finally negotiations were completed with a firm in Saratoga, Florida, whose business was raising all sorts of weird pets from rattlesnakes to alligators. He recommended great horned owls at $12 a head but Marietta took common screech owls because they were only $3.50.

Quoting from the article, here's what happened:

Mr. Wellons let it be known that the flat-faced rescuers were on the way to raise the siege. Then the battlefield was prepared by the fire department, which shinned up the trees, placing perches for the owls and tins to hold food and water, also leashes made to tie the owls to the perches so there would be no desertion in the face of the enemy.

The date for the decisive battle was set for the following Friday evening and, besides the natives, others from far and wide assembled to watch and make bets. In came the martins to circle around the town and roost in the park trees as usual, but no owls.

A delegation called on Mr. Wellons to ask if his soldiers were showing the white feather and learned that it was even worse. The army had vanished entirely on its way up from Florida so the battle was off indefinitely.

Finally the mystery was solved. "Wrong-way" Corrigan had nothing on those owls which turned up in Marietta, Ohio, instead of Marietta, Georgia. (Corrigan was an aviator who left the east coast of the U.S. to fly to the west coast, but ended up in Europe instead.) The Ohio city's fathers were astonished because they had no martin problem. They refused to accept consignment of owls, C.O.D. Rerouted to the correct Marietta, the owls arrived in their normal condition of unruffled dignity. The attack was then scheduled for the second evening following, but a queer thing happened.

Just as if the intelligence department of the martin hordes had informed them of the presence of the new enemy, the martin army of occupation suddenly and mysteriously disappeared, leaving only about a hundred as rear guard and observers. Up went the owls to their perches and off went the rear guard of martins as fast as they could flap their wings. But they left unhappy memories.

Long before I joined the staff, the *Cobb County Times* was recognized as one of the best weekly newspapers in the U.S. and had received several awards attesting to this fact. These included the Mergenthaler Awards in 1917-1918 for outstanding typography and the Casey All-American, 1935-1936 and Casey All-Time All-American in 1936-1937. Georgia press Association awards were the Hal M. Stanley Trophy, 1933, and the Trox Bankston Trophy, 1936. All of these reflected the high quality apparent in every aspect of the newspaper.

In 1938, when Publisher Brumby received notice of the *Times* winning an unprecedented four first-place awards in National

Editorial Association competition, jubilation spread throughout the organization. Otis, of course, was elated and soon headed for White Sulphur Springs, West Virginia, for the awards ceremony. Upon his return, he was greeted by his nephew, Robert Fowler, who although an adolescent, displayed a keen interest in newspapers, especially his uncle's. (Years later, Robert would purchase the *Gwinnett Daily News*, build it up into an outstanding paper, then sell it to the *New York Times* in a multi-million dollar deal.)

Otis and Robert were pictured in the *Times*, with Robert holding the trophies and Otis by his side, beaming.

The four NEA awards were: General Excellence, General Excellence in Typography, Newspaper Production, and Best Use of Illustrative Material.

It was just prior to this that Otis had hired Gilbert P. Farrar, nationally-known typography expert to restyle the *Times* following the then current trend throughout the country. We had heard Mr. Farrar speak at the Georgia Press Institute in Athens, and we knew he was restyling the *Atlanta Journal*. Otis was so impressed he invited him to come to Marietta for a couple of days (at a cost of $600 per day, according to rumor) and completely change the appearance of the *Times*. This meant adopting a new style altogether, or a more modern dress, as it was described. Headlines were placed flush left, instead of the traditional style of gradually indenting them. The page makeup was radically changed also with larger size heads extending over more columns, and the type strung out underneath making it easier for the eye to follow.

Since I was responsible for makeup, I worked very closely with Mr. Farrar and learned more about typography and makeup than I had ever learned previously in so short a period. And it was up-to-date knowledge of an important subject. (This would prove to be very helpful when in 1950 I joined the printing firm of Higgins-McArthur in Atlanta and came under the tutelage of Richard N. McArthur, widely known as a type designer and typographer throughout this country and in Europe.)

RESTYLER AND PUBLISHER TALK IT OVER

Here are Otis A. Brumby, publisher of the Times, and Gilbert P. Farrar, typographical expert, discussing features of the restyled makeup of the Times, which appears this week for the first time
in its modern new dress. Mr. Farrar, who recently redesigned a leading Atlanta daily, is shown
in the pressroom of the Times pointing out to Mr. Brumby advantages in legibility and general
attractiveness brought about by the change. The Times is the first weekly newspaper to employ
expert help in restyling.—Staff photo by Edmund Hughes for Loudermilk Studio.

    Known mainly today as the birthplace of film star Julia Roberts
and the current home of her mother, Smyrna in 1938 was a sleepy
town of several thousand inhabitants spread out over a large area
of southern Cobb County. In October of that year, the calm was
shattered on two successive nights when hundreds of angry
mobsters gathered on the main street of Smyrna to protest the
brutal axe-handle slaying of a 66-year-old retired white farmer
and his daughter, age 26, by a black man.

    This resulted in headline news across the nation. A visitor re-
turning from Chicago reported seeing a headline on the front
page of one newspaper proclaiming in big bold type: "Race Riot
Smyrna, Ga."

The murders occurred in the early morning of October 16 when the farmer, his daughter, and her 9-year-old son were attacked in their home near Smyrna. The mother and her father were slain and the boy left for dead. Badly wounded, he managed to survive and crawl a hundred yards through the countryside and report the tragedy to neighbors. The boy identified the murderer as Willie Drew Russell, 31, who was quickly apprehended and placed in the Fulton County jail, then moved to Tattnall State Prison for safekeeping after receiving threats against him.

At dusk that day, the mob began gathering, and by nightfall, hundreds of angry men were milling about in Atlanta Street in Smyrna.

Frustrated by the knowledge that the murderer had been moved to the state prison, the mob grew surly and resorted to violence against innocent black people. They pulled them from buses and street cars and beat them. They stopped black-occupied automobiles and did the same. They even burned a black schoolhouse and set fire to a church.

As Chess and I would write in the editorial, "They violated every fundamental right guaranteed under the Constitution of the United States."

Chess and I visited the scene a couple of times for a first-hand report and were appalled by the senseless violence. After our first visit, we returned to the office, sat down and, with grim determination, batted out the editorial titled "You Yellow Rats." Chess manned the typewriter and did most of the writing, but I supplied the headline and made other suggestions which were followed.

As an interesting sidelight, it happened that Otis Brumby had suffered an attack of painful rheumatism that night and was being carried by ambulance to a Marietta hospital. His ambulance was stopped by the mobsters and he was delayed getting to the hospital for treatment. After this experience, he endorsed our editorial even more than he normally might have, saying "take off your gloves, boys."

Meanwhile, Cobb police had arrested 17 mob suspects and placed them in jail on a charge of "malicious mischief."

Being responsible for all news coverage for the newspaper, it was my job to report the happenings, supposedly in an objective manner. This was difficult because of my strong anti-mob feelings. Also, I needed to find a fresh angle to the story since the Atlanta newspapers and the national news services had covered it extensively. So, just before deadline, I grabbed my camera and headed for the Cobb County jail where the suspects were being held.

There I approached Deputy Sheriff George McMillan and said I wanted to interview the prisoners. George laughed and said, "Ed, you can't do that. Those men are scared, not knowing what's going to happen to them. They won't talk. Several Atlanta reporters and wire service men have been here, but they won't see them."

At my insistence, the deputy agreed to give me a chance to interview them. So, with no definite plan in mind, I accompanied the deputy down to the cells where they were held. As I approached one cell, several bedraggled men came to the door with questioning looks in their faces.

Then an idea flashed into my mind.

"I want to get a picture of all you guys who are not guilty," I said.

That did it. One of the men, apparently their leader, said, "You can take my picture. I'm not guilty." Another said, "Me too. I wasn't even there."

Murmurs of general assent followed throughout the cell. So the deputy unlocked the door and I went in, lined them against a wall and took the photograph. They readily identified themselves, and I interviewed them while writing down their names and addresses.

The same thing occurred at a nearby cell where the others were being held. I used the same ploy and they were just as cooperative, and seemed to be relieved to be able to talk to someone about their plight.

The pictures appeared on the front page of the *Times* the next day with the heading, "Not Guilty, They Chorus." The caption read, "These men arrested in connection with the rioting at

"NOT GUILTY,' THEY CHORUS

Smyrna, say they are not guilty. However, Sheriff's deputies say most of them were ringleaders."

Our editorial, titled "You Yellow Rats," ran just under the pictures.

It should be revealed that following publication of that issue, Chess and I received veiled threats of personal harm, but fortunately, nothing of that nature developed.

Otis Brumby's reaction to the mob violence was captured the next week in his front page column Jambalaya, which he dictated to a stenographer from his hospital bed. Publisher Brumby expressed himself in his usual forthright manner, leaving no doubt as to his true feeling. Here several paragraphs from that are reproduced exactly as they appeared in the October 27, 1938 issue.

JAMBALAYA
By Otis A. Brumby

From my hospital bed I have managed to keep fairly close in touch with local happenings and like everybody else in Cobb County, and surrounding territory, chief interests have been centered around the deplorable demonstration of mob violence which, most unfortunately, found its way into one of the most peaceful communities in the South, last week.

Knowing, as I do, that our neighboring little city of Smyrna is normally one of the most law abiding communities in the state and that her citizens are rated as being among the finest in the country, it is doubly regretable that the tiny spot they occupy on the huge map of our country has, through no fault of theirs, been smeared in such a manner and that months and years will be required before that smear can be erased.

Smyrna Gets Bad Publicity

This thought had a great deal to do with the stand your favorite newspaper took las week in condemning the actions of that mob. The fact that our friendly and neighborly fellow citizens of Smyrna were not responsible for the actions of that mob and that the eyes of the nation were unjustly focused on their city made us all the more determined to use every facility at our command to let the outside world know that the real citizens of Smyrna and Cobb County had no sympathy whatever for the small handful or rowdies who took it upon themselves to establish in the minds of the people of the United States such an unfair picture.

That the stand taken by the TIMES met with the whole hearted approval and endorsement of the real people of Cobb County is manifested in the many letters of commendation we have received. Literally hundreds of people have taken it upon themselves to either write, phone or drop by our offices to express their approval and to voice the hope that this newspaper would continue to encourage our law enforcement officers towards a just and satisfactory conclusion of this unfortunate situation.

Publisher Directed Stand

As a matter of record only, I want it distinctly understood that as owner and publisher of the TIMES that the editorial policy we took in this matter was solely at my directions. My reason for making this statement here is simply the fact that word has reached me that members of my staff have been threatened, in a very round-about way, with personal injury. While they are thoroughly capable of taking care of themselves I feel justified in making the statement that the responsiblity of the TIMES policy, in this instance, is entirely mine and that if vengeance of any type is to be directed towards any member of the TIMES staff it should be directed to me personally.

As a matter of record, too, let it be recorded that the TIMES hasn't in any way changed its attitude.

We feel, just as we did last week, that justice must prevail. That law and order is most sacred with 99 per cent of the people of Cobb County and that we voice the sentiment of that majority when we express the hope that the guilty will be punished in accordance with the law and that the innocent parties will be exonerated and their names cleansed in every way possible.

In the aftermath of all the furor, Willie Drew Russell was tried and found guilty of first degree murder by a jury in Cobb Superior Court and sentenced to die. He was electrocuted a few months later.

As for the mob suspects, they were released from jail after posting bonds of $2,500 each. All of them were indicted by the Cobb County Grand Jury during its next term. Then one was tried and found not guilty of the misdemeanor charge. None of the other cases ever reached trial and the charges were eventually dismissed, or "laid aside," as the prosecuting attorney described it.

All during this period, the newspaper continued to be community service oriented and we all contributed to several worthwhile causes and endeavors. One of these that I took part in and enjoyed was the Soapbox Derby. Its sponsors were the Cogs club, a social and service organization to which I belonged, Chevrolet Motor Co., and the *Times*. I worked with the local Chevrolet dealer, James T. Anderson, in directing the project. It was a national program for boys 14 and younger. They built their own soapbox racers and competed locally. Then the winners would race in the state finals in Atlanta, and the state finalists would vie for the national championship in Akron.

The Marietta race, on a steep hill on Canton Road, attracted several thousand spectators. However, our winner - nine-year-old Richard Crowder, the youngest boy in the race - failed to place in Atlanta.

Otis Brumby displayed a special interest in the Marietta race and took numerous photographs during the various heats, several of which were published in the *Times*, with due credit given to him in the captions.

The *Times* also sponsored a countywide marble tournament for young boys which Editor Abernathy helped supervise and promote. It, too, was highly successful and helped build goodwill for the newspaper.

Another worthwhile *Times* promotion was sponsorship of an annual cooking school. This three-day event, held at the Strand Theatre on Marietta's city square, was conducted by experts in culinary arts and drew women from throughout Cobb County.

In May of 1939 came news that resulted in my temporary promotion to acting editor. At this time, it was announced that Chess was the recipient of a $2,500 Rosewald Fellowship award, which necessitated his being away for a year. This meant I would succeed him during this period as editor and advertising manager.

The award was a well deserved tribute to Chess and his ability, and, naturally, I was quite pleased. Otis was almost ecstatic, not only because of his personal regard for Chess, but because it reflected favorably on the newspaper.

The award was to enable the editor to pursue investigation of "the possibility of developing mutually beneficial trade relations between the South and South America, and to undertake, at the same time, a study of various Latin American newspapers."

Scene at the Abernathy's homecoming with Martha and Chess shown at left center of photo. Otis Brumby (in hat) is directly behind Chess, and his wife, Elisabeth, is at extreme right. Jimmy Carmichael (with cane) and wife, Frances, are at left of Abernathys. I'm second from left, and Warren Duffee is peering over Frances Carmichael's head. Others are family members, including my aunt and uncle, Mayme and Homer McDonald.

Just before Chess departed, Warren Duffee, an Emory University alumnus, was hired to take over the news desk and his name as News Editor was placed under mine on the masthead. Of course, Chess' name as editor remained under Publisher Brumby's.

Warren, although younger and less experienced, was well qualified for the job, being a journalism graduate and having worked for a time on his hometown newspaper in Laurel, Mississippi. He also had served as acting director of the Emory news bureau. (After leaving the *Times*, Warren joined the United Press bureau in Washington, D.C. and remained there for many years as one of the top news men of that organization.)

Fortunately, Warren was dependable and capable, since my new duties were demanding and required all of my attention. This was especially true in selling and handling advertising, which was entirely new to me. But, Chess had attempted to tutor me before he left, and I soon learned to cope with some of the abundant problems inherent in the advertising business. It was a case of sink or swim, and, for a while, I did a little of both.

Not to be outdone by Otis and Chess, in the issue of May 9, 1939, I began my attempt at writing a column, I named the column "HUGHES VIEWS," which was a tip-off as to its nature. Nevertheless, I continued writing the column until I left Marietta for Army service two and a half years later. The writing had to have improved in quality as I gained experience, but just for laughs, I present here the first three paragraphs of my initial effort:

> Ships embark on their maiden voyage... birds poise on the edge of their nest and then drop off into space for their initial flight... actors make their debut from behind brilliant footlights... all of which is just a round-about way of saying this is the writer's first attempt at doing a column. And, now it's more or less boss' orders.
>
> Since coming to Marietta and launching my journalism career some two years ago - then somewhat fearfully - with the *Times*, we have watched with admiration and humble respect as Boss Brumby sits down each week on

Thursday afternoon just before the paper goes to press and bats out his brainchild "Jambalaya," usually within an hour's time and with the utmost ease. Then we've seen Editor Abernathy start his column, "Now I Like That — ," about a year ago, and watched him dash it out week by week, without any hesitation or effort, and between answering phone calls and attending to other business. Now the boss has suggested the idea of our trying to do a column - one not like his, and not like Chess', but different. It's hard to imagine such a thing after the thorough coverage of people and events you get in the other two each week. But, anyway, here goes.

(Today, that kind of writing doesn't have any marketable value, and wouldn't get you a fifty cent bagel in a New York deli.)

The remainder of the column was mostly trivia, interlaced with human interest and humor. This included the date list for the Cogs dance and a plug for the upcoming local production of the operetta, "The Pirates of Penzance." Of course, I had an interest in both of these, since I would attend the Cogs dance and was singing in the chorus of the musical as a lusty pirate.

Later, Chess and I would carry on a friendly feud in our columns about the use of "we" or "I" pronouns in referring to ourselves. He preferred the "I" and I the "we." Each defended his position in the columns we wrote, and other people took sides. Chess said the "I" was more direct and natural. I defended the "we," saying it was wider and therefore easier to hide behind than the skinny "I," and offered more protection from irate readers. I also said its use was more in keeping with journalistic tradition, since all newspaper editorials employed the plural personal pronoun.

One person who commented on our "feud" was Olin Miller in his column on the editorial page of the *Atlanta Journal*. Here's an excerpt from his regular feature, "Quaint Tales From Georgia Quills:"

"We" and "I" trouble: "Recently we made mention here of the scrap Chess Abernathy, editor of the Cobb County Times (Marietta), and Edmund Hughes, managing editor of the same paper, were having concerning the use of "we" and "I" in editorial matter. Somehow we overlooked the fact that Edmund is not only a columnist, but also managing editor (please forgive us, Edmund), and we said something about the danger a columnist exposes himself to when he chunks rocks at an editor. Edmund contends that a managing editor ought to have a little more right than a columnist to abuse an editor, and we'll concede he's right, but at the same time it would be our advice that even a managing editor should sort of pull his punches when he spars with an editor in chief.

(Please note that Miller himself used the "we" pronoun.) Later, in another column, Miller quoted again from my column:

ON GOOD FOOTING
Marietta boasts according to Edmund Hughes in Otis Brumby's Cobb County Times, of a citizen names Jess James, which is pretty tough on him, because of alleged jests, quips, witticisms and whatnots on his cognomen. Mr. Hughes reports that Mr. James is mad. We mean angry, though nobody down South ever says "angry" when he means "mad" or viva voce, if that's the term. Our Dorean language is a bit rusty.
Anyway, it appears that Mr. James ordered, accepted and paid for a pair of shoes guaranteed to be size 13 1/2, and when he tried them on they proved to be size 14, so his tootsies wobbled around in them. Mr. James asserted that it was the first time in his life he's ever found shoes too large for him.
Mr. James, it might be said, is assistant agricultural agent and keeps the 4-H boys well in line. Who couldn't, with a 13 1/2 foot staring them in the face – or elsewhere.

Another popular columnist who commented on my material was Dudley Glass in the old *Atlanta Georgian*, a Hearst newspaper. Here's what he wrote:

AMUSING INCIDENT: "A Mariettan told us of this amusing little incident. It seems a lady, a former Mariettan, had parked her car on an Atlanta street recently and

while waiting for another person, was idly day-dreaming. Suddenly the car door was opened and a strange young man reached in and without a word slapped her twice, severely. Then the gentleman (?) looked her squarely in the face and departed hastily, saying 'Oh, I beg your pardon, I thought you were my wife.'" – Edmund Hughes, in the Cobb County Times (Marietta).
The use of the question mark after "gentleman" in the foregoing paragraph is apt. No gentleman would slap a woman without first making sure she was his wife, and a first-class gentleman wouldn't do it then, except under extremely extenuating circumstances. One man to whom we showed a clipping for the foregoing paragraph said a man was foolish to slap his wife in an automobile anyway. "A fellow can't get a good, wide swing at 'er in a car," he explained.

With the fighting intensifying in Europe and war clouds billowing over Asia, it soon became apparent that I could be ordered to active army duty at any time. My status as a reserve officer meant that I likely would be among the first to be called. I didn't dwell on this - I just accepted it as a strong possibility - but I did follow the war news closely.

By now, Otis and I had become close personal friends. He complimented me on my work and provided strong encouragement.

One afternoon he invited me to go with him to his home on Rottenwood Creek in eastern Cobb County and spend the night while he awaited the birth of his first child at a hospital in Atlanta.

Otis A. Brumby, Junior and Senior, shown with young Otis at an early age.

I knew his wife, Elisabeth, was expecting, and I readily complied with his request. That night Otis cooked us a delicious steak diner and I had an enjoyable time just being with him. We went to bed early, and the next morning he called the hospital and learned that he had a son. Naturally, he was elated and rushed to the hospital for a first glimpse of his offspring.

(Today, Otis, Jr. heads a multi-million dollar publishing empire, which he, with the help of his mother, founded and developed after the death of Otis, Sr. in the early 1950s. It is anchored by the *Marietta Daily Journal* and now has a total of 29 community newspapers in a chain called the Neighbor Newspapers. These are circulated throughout Cobb and surrounding counties.)

Now for an almost unbelievable happening that changed my life - I was duped into singing the male lead in the operetta, "The Merry Widow."

For background: the Marietta Junior Welfare League sponsored a musical event each year, employing local talent, for the benefit of charity. Director of these offerings was Tom Brumby, nephew of Otis, Sr., who was employed at the Brumby Chair factory (later known for manufacturing the Brumby Rocker, made famous by JFK while he was president).

I had sung in the chorus of two of the musicals, including the "Pirates of Penzance," as related previously, and my background was strictly choral or group singing. I had sung in the church choir at Bolton and with the Glee Club at Georgia, but I had never sung a solo and could not read a note of music. I often regretted that I had not accepted my sister's offer to teach me, not only to read music but to play the piano as well.

One morning Tom Brumby called me at the *Times*' office and asked that I come by his home near the chair factory to see him during the lunch hour. I did so and he informed me that a new operetta production was being planned and that he wanted me to understudy a small part. When I protested, he assured me that no solo singing would be involved.

He sat down at the piano and began playing a selection. Looking over his shoulder, I could see the score was "The Merry Widow," Franz Lehar's classic operetta. He was playing the familiar Merry

Widow waltz and, before I realized it, I was singing. This led to Tom playing other selections of the music for the part of Prince Danilo, romantic male lead of the operetta.

I was hooked. The music was delightful and I enjoyed the singing. Tom suggested that I come by often at lunch time. This I did for several weeks. Soon I realized that I had learned (memorized) the entire score. Tom still reassured me: "no solos."

Then came the time for the first practice session of the principals and chorus. Here the Merry Widow made her initial appearance. She was Frances Campbell, a professional singer from Atlanta, with whom Tom worked while directing the choir at St. Phillips Cathedral where she was the paid soprano soloist.

Of course, she had an excellent voice and could read the musical score with ease. I was almost overwhelmed, realizing that Tom, although with the best of intentions, had conned me into learning the part and fully expected me to sing opposite so accomplished a singer. I almost rebelled, but Tom convinced me I was capable of singing the part, which included solos, duets, quartets, and even octets. Besides the singing, the role required that I learn a great deal of dialogue as well. Also, I had to dance with the protagonist to the strains of the Merry Widow waltz.

Realizing all of this, I had nightmares throughout the rehearsal period of several weeks.

Finally came the night of the performance. By then, I was almost overcome by anxiety, even though I had rehearsed the part until it was second nature. My first appearance was on stage alone singing a solo about going off to Maxims and flirting and dancing, with the French girls at that Paris establishment. I remember some of their names: Lolo, Dodo, Margo, Frou Frou, Fifi, Mimi. Somehow I got through that opening number and gained enough confidence to continue. At the end, I was actually enjoying it and wishing for more.

The performance was well received by the jam-packed audience, and I joined with other cast members in celebration after the final curtain. These included the Merry Widow, nee Frances Campbell. By then, she and I had become infatuated with each other, despite some temperamental outburst by her during the

MEET 'THE MERRY WIDOW'!

The show was Franz Lehar's "The Merry Widow." The place was the Atlanta Woman's Club Auditorium. The time was a fortnight ago, and the audience was... well, it was enchanted. The performance was put on by the Junior Welfare League of Marietta, GA, a group of amateurs who produce a similar show every year simply because they like to sing and act, and because they have a whale of a good time doing both. In this scene, Sonia, the Merry Widow (Frances Campbell) greets Prince Danilo (Edmund Hughes). She sings, "For when a man would wed a girl in my own native land, he doesn't call her star and pearl and want to kiss her hand. Says he, 'Let us get married now, we both are growing big. My father has a cow, and your mother has a pig.'"

Names of the Can-Can girls were Lolo, Dodo, Jou-Jou, Frou-Frou, Clo-Clo, Margot, Fifi and Mimi. These three are Dot Montgomery, Lucile Dennison and Jane Kiser - doing a dance number.

early rehearsals. Simply stated, our characters fell in love - and so did we. The drama and excitement engendered by the roles, as well as the plot itself, created a romantic aura that would not be denied.

The next day the Atlanta newspapers carried glowing reviews and actually praised my performance, among others, after pointing out this was my first experience at solo singing and disclosing my inability to read music.

Two months later we repeated the production for two successive nights in Atlanta at the Atlanta Woman's Club Auditorium, again under auspices of the Marietta Junior Welfare League, for charity. These performances were a sell-out, aided by promotional photographs and news stories appearing in the Atlanta newspapers.

The Marsovian peasant girls entertained the royalty. The girls are Rossie Gilmore, Jane Kiser, Lucile Dennison, Ruth Mitchell, Dot Montgomery and Margaret Branch.

Tom Brumby played the organ for the performance, assisted by Mrs. W.E. Oettinger. Mr. Brumby sang the entire libretto under his breath.

"Every touch of fingers tells me what I know - says for you, it's true, it's true, you love me so!" Everybody knew that Sonia, the Merry Widow, and Price Danio would wed.

But the most complete coverage came two weeks afterwards when a full page of photos was published in the Sunday rotogravure section of the *Atlanta Journal*, including lovely can-can dancers and lusty so-called peasant girls cavorting about the stage. It was no secret that some of the young ladies were both can-can dancers and peasant girls, changing costumes from one act to another.

Tom Brumby was pictured seated at the organ while directing. The cutline stated that Tom sang the entire libretto under his breath while the show was in progress.

The Atlanta performances were on February 20-21. In mid-March, all thoughts of music and singing were dismissed from my mind when I received orders to report for military duty. The date for reporting was April 1, and the station, the Reception Center at Fort Oglethorpe, Georgia, near Chattanooga.

It happened that Chess Abernathy was leaving the *Times* at about the same time to become alumni secretary of Emory University, and Otis Brumby waxed eloquent in a column about us. He wrote, in part:

"Over on the editorial page, where the columns of my two associates, Edmund Hughes and Chess Abernathy, appear there is a sad note. In Hughes Views, Ed sings his swan song. He is getting away Monday to report to Uncle Sam's army up at Chattanooga where he will go into training for a year - or longer. Ed is a reserve officer. Our youthful editor, Chess Abernathy, expresses his sorrow over leaving Marietta and our organization - to take up his duties with Emory University in the next few weeks."

"I will miss both of these fine boys - we have been great pals in our work - we have had our ups and downs and gotten along together swell. Once even our youthful Mr. Abernathy referred to me as being a 'veteran' and 'venerable' - in spite of such things, I have forgiven him long ago. So it's been all these years."

In our respective farewell columns, Chess and I engaged in some emotional language to express mutual appreciation for our personal working relationship over several years.

Here's an excerpt from my column: "This is to better let him know we've thoroughly enjoyed our association with him, and to show, in a measure, our affection for him, and to wish him the very best of luck in his new position at Emory University."

Chess wrote in a similar vein about me: "Maybe this little column will help Ed to know how we feel about him. Best of luck to a tried and true member of the fourth estate who goes forth, along with other Americans, to perform the last full measure of patriotic devotion, if need be... "

In his column the following week, Otis went further, becoming even more emotional in discussing my departure and praising me in fulsome terms. Much of this I now attribute to patriotic fervor and my leaving under such circumstances. I debated about including here what he wrote, but a consensus among several of my close friends determined I should do so.

So, putting modesty aside, here it is:

JAMBALAYA

By Otis A. Brumby

He Is In The Army Now

Uncle Sam reached out and put his finger right down in the midst of our organization last week. They need good men in the new army they are training, so Edmund Hughes, our associate editor and general utility man, was ordered to report to Ft. Oglethorpe, near Chattanooga. He was a reserve officer, having been in the military unit over at the University. He is now in the army – a first lieutenant. He left Tuesday morning and checked in before sundown at the army post.

I hated to see Ed go. For some time the order had been expected and though I had been preparing myself for the separation and knew the order was coming I hated to see it come for more reasons than one. For pure unadulterated selfish reasons I hated to see Ed leave. He had been old man Handy Andy himself around our office for several years. He came to us a green cub reporter and developed rapidly. On the city news desk he handled his work faithfully, accurately and efficiently. He made friends rapidly and his sources of news contacts were many and loyal to him. He developed into a first rate news photographer, he wrote editorials, his own column and did countless other things necessary to make the TIMES a better newspaper from week to week.

Pinch Hitter for Chess

When Chess Abernathy, our editor, was awarded his Rosenwald Fellowship that took him away for a year, Ed stepped right in to hold down that responsible job. How well he did the work is reflected in the success of the newspaper during those twelve months. He became a good ad salesman, and brought in a nice run of business. In truth he made quite a reputation for himself and proved his ability in more ways than one. When Chess came back, Ed took over job printing and here his real talents came to the surface. In the meantime he contributed articles to the newspaper and kept up his personal column, Hughes Views. He never forgot he was first and last a newspaper man – a reporter – always on the job – day or night – when a story came under his observations. He loved his work and endeared himself to every member of our organization by his earnestness and his enthusiasm.

A Real Friend

Another reason I hate to see Ed go is one of friendship. He has been a pal all the time he has been here with our organization. He has accompanied me on many trips to conventions and the like. He always was a gentleman under any circumstances. He was the kind of fellow you are proud to have along with you. He was mighty good company. He never complained about the work put on him and no matter what the assignment was he tackled it with enthusiasm and got results. He was a team man always and never thought about himself – it was everything for the paper and for me. I could go on and on and tell you many fine things about him – but this is not an obituary it is just a few well-deserved words that I want to get in print while he is around to read them – and I want his legion of friends to know just how much I think of him – and how much I hate to see him go – even on such a necessary mission.

It has been a gratifying experience to me to see Ed develop from a green cub reporter to a first-class, all-around newspaper man. I am already missing him a lot – I am going to miss him more. I hope Uncle Sam will appreciate his worth. Since this thing had to happen we here at the TIMES are proud that Ed is in the army – we know he will make a good soldier – and when the end of his training period comes – and Uncle Sam turns him back to civilian life – his place is waiting for him – and, too, we will all be mighty glad to see him back.

By now Frances and I were dating regularly, and we both dreaded the separation resulting from my military service. However, that problem was resolved by a long distance phone call. Three days after my arrival at Fort Oglethorpe, I was paged that night at a wrestling match I was watching with two fellow-officers at the city auditorium in Chattanooga. It was Frances on the telephone from Atlanta saying she wanted to get married right away. Of course, I agreed and hurried plans were made for the ceremony at St. Philips Cathedral, with the full choir singing and Tom Brumby directing. The wedding date was April 13, 1941, with Dean Raimundo de Ovies officiating.

GROWING UP TOO FAST, TOO SOON

"All aboard." That cry of the train conductor found me visibly shaken while slumped on the Pullman car seat. Minutes earlier I had boarded this Chattanooga Choo Choo — recalling a popular song title of that day — in the Terminal Station at Chattanooga, Tennessee.

The date: May 11, 1942.

I, First Lieutenant Edmund C. Hughes, Infantry, U.S. Army, had orders to proceed from my station at Fort Oglethorpe, Georgia, near Chattanooga, to the Port of Embarkation, San Francisco, for "extended field duty outside the continental limits of the United States." I would have gasped had I known how extended that duty would become.

Having just left a tearful wife and a three-week-old daughter, I braced myself to accept whatever lay ahead. Adventure was the key. That sustained me — the thought of new places, new people, and the unknown. My orders had arrived two weeks before, just after the birth of Corrie, my first child. To me, Port of Embarkation had an exciting ring. I knew embark meant boarding a ship, but the unknown destination gave an added fillip. Who could have foretold that almost three and a half years later I would crouch in a crowded gun turret aboard the battleship Missouri and watch as two grim-faced Japanese delegates, along with several high-ranking allied military representatives, signed the surrender documents ending World War II? (Not that I had contributed much to Japan's surrender.) Nor could anyone have imagined that I would meet and talk with General Douglas MacArthur. Or that before I left Japan in October 1945, MacArthur would personally present me with a signed photograph, inscribed with these words: "To Major Hughes With Cordial Regard Tokyo, 1945 Douglas MacArthur."

Nor could anyone have conceived of the other memorable experiences I would have. During the course of that time — through necessity — I would grow up too fast, too soon.

As I lounged on the Pullman seat, waiting for the train to pull out, I reflected on army life, as well as my life in general.

I disliked the army from the beginning. Called to active duty April 1, 1941, I was assigned to the Reception Center at Fort Oglethorpe where I served as a classification officer for more than a year. This meant I was in charge of individual interviewing and testing of newly-inducted draftees from throughout Tennessee to determine their fitness for different jobs and what branch of service would be most suitable for them.

I had obtained my commission as a second lieutenant through ROTC at the University of Georgia in 1937. Following graduation with a journalism degree, I attended a two-week Officers Reserve Corps training camp and thus automatically became eligible for advancement to first lieutenant after a three-year waiting period. This promotion came less than a year before I received orders to report for duty.

Following college, my life as managing editor of a weekly newspaper in Marietta, Georgia, had been unhurried and uncomplicated. I was given that imposing title immediately upon being hired. The job was long on hours, but short on pay. The salary started at $15 a week. Yet, I thrived on it and found complete satisfaction in the work — from reporting and editing the news to writing the editorials. I even found time to write a weekly personal column on whatever subjects I chose. My efforts were not of Pulitzer Prize caliber, it should be noted here. However, in 1938, the newspaper, the *Cobb County Times*, did received national recognition, winning an unprecedented four first place awards in annual competition sponsored by the National Editorial Association, including one for General Excellence. Later, I became acting editor and advertising manager when the editor won a Rosenwald Fellowship and traveled in South America for a year. Then I became assistant to the president of the company and learned something of the business and technical sides of printing, which stood me in good stead after the war.

As managing editor of weekly   Two years later, while working as
newspaper, 1937.   acting editor.

Without question, I was the rawest and greenest first lieutenant in the service. Not having studied or thought about anything connected to the army for almost four years, I felt completely out of sync with the military. And I knew this was evident.

Here I was a small town guy plopped down in the middle of a military establishment. I felt I was lucky to have a little rank, being a first lieutenant. (The post commander was only a lieutenant colonel.) But, I believe another meaning of the word "rank" would have been more appropriate as applied to me.

This feeling was heightened when for the first week at the Reception Center I was totally ignored and not given any assignment by the commanding officer, Captain Ivan Ward. During that time I sat around and read books on army regulations... and sweated... and waited. My suffering ended when Captain Ward called me into his office and explained and apologized. It happened that following my physical examination at the post hospital, my records through error had been switched with another officer's who had tested positive for tuberculosis. Thinking I had the disease, Captain Ward said he felt it unnecessary to give me an assignment since I would be admitted to a hospital for treatment and probably dismissed from the service. As a precaution, I was re-tested and the X-ray was negative.

The ordeal had been made worse by my feelings of guilt over being a pack-a-day smoker, with a slight cough. I weighed 146 pounds with a height of five feet eleven inches. Yet, sad to relate, I did not quit smoking until several years after the war.

Army life was not suited to my temperament. I was an individualist. I liked freedom of thought and expression — and action. I hated the discipline of having to conform to rules and regulations. I also hated being told what to do without question. I still do today. It's against my independent nature.

Marriage compounded my problems. I had married less than two weeks after entering the service — another commitment for which I was ill prepared. My wife, Frances, was considerate and understanding, but the memories of those early days are troubling to me still.

Overshadowing all else during this trying period had been the death of my father, Miles Alexander Hughes, at age 60. He died March 27, 1941 — just four days before I reported for army duty — from a coronary thrombosis after suffering with a heart condition for several years. This was my first experience as an adult in dealing with the death of a close relative. As with most young men, my father was my idol. I revered and respected him, even though there was never much show of affection between us by words or actions. To me, he personified all that was good. He was a true Christian and was recognized as such.

As her youngest offspring, I attempted to console my grieving mother, Annie Lee McDonald Hughes, but with limited success. He had been her life — except for her love of an occasional shopping trip to downtown Atlanta. She survived him by more than 26 years, dying peaceably in her sleep June 5, 1967 at age 81.

Because a younger brother of mine, Miles, Jr., had died in infancy, mother had often turned to me for solace. She was my companion, my mentor, my unfailing supporter. I only wish I had lived up to her expectations for me. I cried openly at her funeral.

A diary I began keeping the day I left Chattanooga for overseas expresses my feelings better than I could today. Here's part of what I wrote in the initial entry, my first night on the train, while hurtling through the countryside:

"Today marks a new beginning for me. It's an opportunity for good, if I make it so. My greatest desire is to apply myself in helping to defeat the Japanese, no matter where I end up serving, so I can return the soonest possible time to my family and friends and enjoy a normal lifestyle out of the army. I am sad to be leaving, but, since I have no choice but to go, I should make the best of it and learn from my experiences."

The three-and-a-half day train trip was tiring and uneventful. The route went through parts of Alabama, Mississippi, Louisiana, Texas, New Mexico and Arizona.

My biggest problem was a lack of personal hygiene due to the absence of bathing facilities on the train.

Diary entry of May 13: "Today was much the same as yesterday. Arrived in Lubbock, Texas, about 10 a.m., without having had breakfast. Went to Hilton Hotel for bath and was permitted to take one in a nice room without charge. Very generous management."

That was my last bath before arriving in San Francisco more than two days later. I probably was the grungiest first lieutenant in the service.

CENSORING — SOMEBODY HAD TO DO IT

All the clamor over military censorship of the media in the more recent Persian Gulf war had me sifting through memories of my experiences while dealing with war correspondents during World War II.

"Daddy, what did you do in the war?"

"I was a censor, son."

That conversation actually never took place, but it could have anytime after my return home from three and a half years of army service as a media censor and public relations officer in the Pacific.

The word censor conjures up a bespectacled ogre, with grim visage, ready to slash beautifully-written copy with quick strokes of a blue pencil. But army regulations decreed that somebody had to do it. At least, we were assigned the duty, and had no choice but to perform in that capacity.

For those of us in public relations, our job was to provide for war correspondents and censor what they wrote. We were entirely responsible for correspondents under our control. We arranged for their food, lodging and transportation in combat areas, as well as facilities for speedy transmission of their dispatches. Out in the field, we ate together, slept together, showered together, partied together, joked together, and sometimes cried together (over the loss of a mutual friend).

Usually, a spirit of camaraderie prevailed, despite the give and take that occurred over the censor's table. Yet, for us, it was a Jekyll and Hyde role. On the one hand, severely cutting or completely prohibiting a particular story could cause great concern to a correspondent. Perhaps a salary increase would be at stake, or at least praise from his editor-boss back in the U.S.

On the other hand, it was incumbent upon us as public relations officers to cater to them and defer to their wishes whenever possible, thus maintaining their goodwill towards us and the command, meaning General MacArthur.

Correspondents were difficult to categorize, but most were dependable and trustworthy. Their job demanded that they be tough and aggressive. They didn't strive to be popular. One too popular usually wasn't doing his job.

Censoring in the early days at Melbourne. Note the quaint furnishings.

War correspondents came in all stripes and dispositions. Handling correspondents was like herding cats, someone said. As with cats, there were different breeds — different temperaments. Some were feisty and antagonistic. They would fight censorship at every turn, as a matter of principle. Jack Turcott, of the *New York Daily News*, fit this description.

A typical New Yorker, with befitting accent, Jack would loudly protest any threat of a censor raising a pencil to his precious copy, no matter how much in violation of the security rules he happened to be. He would scream, rant and rave — usually to no avail.

Then, if the hapless censor persisted, he would demand to be heard by higher authority, no matter at what hour of the day or night. That was his right, and the story in question would be referred to our boss, chief censor Colonel B.A. Tormey, or, even higher, to Brigadier General LeGrande A. Diller, chief of public relations and MacArthur's aide.

In a lighter moment, Turcott once jokingly remarked to me that following the war he would write a book with the title, "I Fought With MacArthur." That title would have been rather appropriate, I thought, not only applying to him, but to some of the others as well.

Other correspondents used sly tactics, like Bryden Taves, United Press bureau chief, attempting to evade censorship with a clever ploy that almost succeeded.

It happened on Christmas Eve night of 1942 as I sat alone at the night shift censorship desk in Brisbane, Australia.

But first, by way of explanation, ostensibly no Marines were under MacArthur's command at that time. However, all Marines of the 1st Division were in Australia for rest and recuperation after the fierce fighting at Guadalcanal. Even though these Marines were seen daily in their distinctive uniform on the streets of Melbourne and Sydney, no mention of their presence was allowed in the overseas press, and a directive to this effect had been issued to all correspondents. This was to prevent the Japanese from knowing their whereabouts, and thus fitting them into the enemy's intelligence network.

On this particular night, about 1:30 Christmas morning, Taves entered the office with what appeared to be a routine, innocuous story of one paragraph about how American servicemen were spending Christmas in Australia. He greeted me cordially, wishing me a Merry Christmas, and smiled as he handed me the typed manuscript.

The story began: "Thousands of soldiers sailors marines thronged the streets of this metropolitan city tonight... "

If that had gone out over the airwaves, as it would have within a few minutes if I had approved it with my censor's stamp, the whole world, including the Japanese, would have learned that the 1st Marine Division was in Australia.

Luckily, despite the lateness of the hour, I reacted in time to delete the word "marines." And, if I hadn't my job as a censor probably would have been terminated.

Yet, except for a reproving glance as I excised the offending word, I never reproached Bryden for his attempt to breach censorship. But I did deal with him more warily thereafter.

This dimly lit scene reflects the atmosphere of an early GHQ press conference with then-Colonel Diller presiding. The time: July 1942. The place: Melbourne, Australia. From left: Diller, Lieutenant Colonel Lehrbas, Lieutenant Baulch, (I'm next), Colonel Howard, Australian PRO officer, and Yates McDaniel, AP bureau chief (who's in "The Haugland Story").

Taves, dapper with a small mustache, later married a well known Australian actress and settled down to as much wedded bliss as the war and his job would allow. Unfortunately, he was killed about a year later in an airplane crash off the coast of New Guinea while on assignment.

"This is Martin Agronsky reporting from somewhere in Australia."

Reading these typewritten words rather than hearing them spoken on the radio was the main shock I experienced my first day as a censor. I had been assigned the job rather hurriedly, and went to work immediately.

After a brief explanation of censorship rules by a fellow officer, I, along with several others in public relations and 20 or so war correspondents, attended a press briefing based on the communique of the day. That was daunting enough.

Then, I was seated at a table to face correspondents, none of whom I had met, filing stories for censorship.

Suddenly, I was aware of a figure leaning over the table. I looked up into the piercing dark eyes of Martin Agronsky. He handed me the script, and in his deep, gravelly voice said, "I need this in a hurry. I go on the air in 20 minutes."

To me, he was a celebrity. Here was a man I had heard at home in many radio news broadcasts from overseas. Yes, he was a celebrity, and I had never expected to be face to face with him.

In that state of awe, I would have approved anything he had written — except maybe if he had disclosed the location of an allied submarine base off the coast of Australia.

Following the war, Agronsky became better known as a television personality, with a weekly panel show of his own for several years. By then, I noted, his dark hair had become sprinkled with gray.

My censoring chores began in Melbourne in July 1942, just after General MacArthur had arrived from the Philippines to take command of the combined Australian and American forces.

I had landed about the same time as MacArthur, but my arrival was greeted with considerably less fanfare than MacArthur's. In fact, I was a "casual" officer, meaning I was not assigned to any particular outfit during the sea voyage from San Francisco to Melbourne.

I tried to be casual, but that was difficult with 600 army nurses aboard. Besides, they cluttered up the seascape, obstructing the view.

Security was tight, especially at night when the ship was entirely blacked out. No lights of any kind were permitted so as not to reveal our presence to a lurking Japanese submarine.

Naturally, friendships quickly developed between nurses and male officers. Each day at twilight twosomes would meet at pre-designated places on shipboard, each with a blanket over an arm. Thereafter, in the total darkness, it required careful footing to avoid stepping on figures sprawled on blankets over the entire huge deck. Just to take a stroll, a refresher course in hopscotching might have been helpful.

Me? Naw — an observer only. I was in no mood for romance, even if invited, having just left a wife and three-week-old daughter at home.

Pictured above are nine of the more than 150 war correspondents accredited to General MacArthur's command during World War II. Some correspondents fought MacArthur's censorship at every turn. Three of the above are written about in my articles that appear here-in. Standing: Earle Crotchett, Universal News; Frank Smith, Chicago Times; Edward Widdis, AP; First Lieutenant Monte Kleban, PR officer; George Folster, NBC; Vern Haugland, AP (see "The Haugland Story'). Seated: Jack Turcott, New York Daily News ; William Courtenay, London Daily Sketch; Lee Van Atta, INS; Don Caswell, UP (also in "The Haugland Story").

Now for the story of how I was selected as a censor.

Some pundit once said "when you think of a time, you remember moments." The time I'm thinking of was when I met Jerry Baulch at a party the hospitable Aussies had for us the night after landing.

Jerry was a personable individual about my age, and we had similar backgrounds. We both had grown up in the South, he in Louisiana, I in Georgia. He had graduated from LSU's journalism school, as I had from the University of Georgia's. Both of us had the rank of first lieutenant.

There the similarity ended. Jerry was called into service while working as a reporter for the Associated Press in Baton Rouge. He already had created a name for himself, I learned later, in covering the assassination of Governor Huey P. Long for AP. I had been employed by a weekly newspaper in Marietta, Georgia, prior to the war.

The moments I remember most about meeting Jerry was how congenial we were from the beginning. He informed me he had been assigned to General Headquarters in public relations and was already serving as a censor. He asked if I would be interested in similar duty, saying they were seeking another person with the necessary qualifications.

Liking Jerry and having no other prospects for a specific assignment, I quickly agreed to be interviewed.

The next morning, bleary-eyed and slightly hung over from the partying the night before, I met Jerry at a downtown office building where MacArthur's headquarters was located.

Approaching the start of winter, it was bitterly cold in Melbourne in early June, as the seasons in Australia are the reverse of ours. I was wearing my "pinks", meaning my winter dress uniform, which derived the name from its trousers with a pinkish tinge. At age 27, I was cocky enough to feel secure and confident. Still, I was awe-struck at the thought of meeting people so closely associated with General MacArthur, whose name had been revered among many of my acquaintances back in Georgia.

LOOKING UP "DOWN UNDER"

"**G**'Day, Mate."

Reading that distinctive greeting in a magazine adver-
tisement recently reminded me this autobiography
would not be complete without offering my impressions of Australia and its people, since I spent two years "down under" during
World War II.

Certainly, that continent and the colorful Aussies have come
alive in so many respects in the intervening years since the war.
Even though I haven't been back, I have noted the enormous
forward strides that have occurred there, from reading periodicals, watching television and viewing movies. Especially is this
progress apparent in the case of movies. That industry has developed and flourished to make Australia one of the most important
movie-making centers of the world. Among the first, "Crocodile
Dundee" caught the public's imagination, and other successes
followed until now it seems there's a new release every month or
so.

Apart from initiating a successful motion picture industry,
Australia has changed and improved in other areas. It is breaking
its outdated ties with England as part of the British empire, and
has changed its monetary system to one based on the dollar rather
than the pound. It also has modified its once stringent immigration
policies.

I landed in Melbourne June 4, 1942, disembarking from the
good ship West Point after the 15-day voyage from San Francisco.

No one could have imagined a more cordial welcome. The
Aussies greeted us like saviors, which in a sense we were. Here
was a continent, roughly the size of the United States, with seven
million inhabitants, the vast majority of whom were women,
children and old folks. Their eligible men had been overseas
fighting in Africa and the Middle East for several years.

From the north, the Japanese posed a real threat to invade Australia, and we knew this was on the minds of the Aussies,

especially after the enemy's abortive air raid on Darwin in the Northern Territory. Shortly afterwards came the fierce fighting by U.S. Marines for Henderson Field on Guadalcanal, which the Japanese, if successful in holding, could use as a base for bombing Port Moresby, New Guinea, only 900 miles away. Being just a few hundred miles from Australia, Port Moresby could have been the springboard for an attempt to conquer the entire continent.

I admit now to have been feeling some trepidation myself, if I had allowed myself to think about it.

Walking a main street of Melbourne with colleague Norm Myers, on left. But not militarily — we're out of step.

In view of this situation, the American troops were a Godsend to the people "down under" and the Aussies showed their appreciation in every way possible. Occasionally I even saw a gray-haired U.S. colonel with an attractive young Australian woman, half his age, on his arm. Saying of the day: "A bird colonel with an eagle on his shoulder can better withstand the rigors of war with a chick on his knee."

By nature, the Aussies were warm and friendly - just like most Americans - but fiercely independent. Also, like Americans. Except for the similarities in language, the Australians resembled us more than they did their British cousins.

A letter to the publisher of the newspaper I had been employed by best expresses my feelings at that time. Here's an excerpt from that letter, published December 10, 1942:

In Brisbane, late 1942.
Still a first lieutenant.

"The Australian, in many ways, is just another American with a peculiar accent, which isn't English, nor is it American. But, on the whole, they are more like southerners in America than northerners or westerners - except in their speech. They have a tendency to clip their words and to end their sentences with a rising inflection in a manner that's almost indescribable."

Please bear in mind this was written more than 59 years ago, before the advent of television and Australian movies.

During my Australian stay I spent several months in each of the three major east coast cities. Sydney was my favorite, I guess, since it was more modern and larger, and more like an American city. But, Melbourne had its charms, with the residents having a more reserved, dignified bearing and who felt closer ties to England. Brisbane, more like a big country town, I liked least of all. Yet, some of its people outdid themselves with friendliness.

Strange to say, I have no desire to revisit that intriguing land "down under," as several of my former associates have done. With most of my old Australian "cobbers" (friends) gone, the trip could only revive poignant memories best forgotten.

THE HAUGLAND STORY

Vern Haugland, a gentle bear of a man, was my favorite among all the war correspondents. Yet, Vern almost cost me my job as a censor and public relations officer on General MacArthur's staff.

Vern, an Associated Press reporter and writer, gave the impression of considerable size and height without being big or tall. He was pleasant to everyone, and possessed a gee whiz-type personality reminiscent of Jimmy Stewart in his movie roles.

The incident involving Vern started on a day in mid-August 1942 when he left on a flight from Townsville, Australia, bound for Port Moresby, New Guinea. At the same time, I was on temporary duty at Townsville.

Here's how I described what happened in a letter to the publisher of the weekly newspaper I had worked for before the war:

Do you remember reading in the newspapers about Vern Haugland, the Associated Press correspondent who was forced to bail out of a plane in New Guinea, was not heard from for about six weeks, but who turned up a few weeks ago nearly dead from hunger and exhaustion? He's fully recovered now, after the worst ordeal I've ever heard of any man surviving. He kept a diary for three or four weeks - as long as he was able - while wandering through the trackless rain forests of the most impenetrable jungle country in the world. How he survived is a miracle.

His diary told how he lived off the scant jungle fare. For weeks, he subsisted on small animals, birds, insects, berries, roots, bark, and foliage from bushes and trees - anything he could find. Finally, he stumbled upon a band of natives (fortunately not headhunting cannibals) who cared for him until missionaries carried him by stretcher to a military hospital at Port Moresby. There he lingered between life and death for days.

His diary was a masterpiece of reporting and provided the basis for one of the best news stories I have read. Certainly, it was the best I have censored.

I have a personal interest in the story, because it happened I was one of the last persons to see Vern before he took off for New Guinea. On this particular day, I had said goodbye to him at the office. Then, shortly afterwards, I had gone back to my hotel. As I was leaving my room I saw Vern hurriedly locking his room door, preparatory to leaving for the airport. His baggage was all about him and he appeared to be having some difficulty getting his door locked. I walked over, shook hands with him, and wished him luck, adding, "Hope you get lots of good stories in New Guinea." He got those stories all right, but suffered as few men have while doing so.

Vern, after several weeks of recuperation, has now fully recovered and regained the nearly 50 pounds he lost. In fact, he recently came back to work, and just tonight presented me with a several hundred word article to censor, which I did before finishing this letter to you.

During Haugland's convalescence, General MacArthur flew to Port Moresby and personally pinned the Silver Star decoration for valor on his pajamas as he lay on a hospital cot.

By this time I had returned to Brisbane, Australia, for regular duty at MacArthur's headquarters. That's when my painful involvement began.

Censorship in Australia operated under a dual arrangement whereby all press stories leaving the country were scrutinized by both U.S. military and Australian government censors. Normally, stories affecting only the military were left to our discretion, and those involving internal affairs were the province of the Australian censors.

We worked side by side with Aussie censors, and we were in agreement on most matters.

These Australian censors were three of our counter-
parts with whom we worked closely. Left to right:
Harold Eather, Tom Foley and Lloyd Clarke. Eather,
deputy chief commonwealth censor, became a personal
friend of mine.

In any event, two stamps - one affixed by a U.S. military censor
and another by one of the Australians - were required before a
news story could be transmitted by beam wireless to various news
media or read by a correspondent in a direct radio broadcast.

The usual censoring procedure was that the stories were submitted to the military censor, and then approved (or not approved)
and passed on to the Australian civilian for his perusal.

The Haugland story was handled on a delayed release basis. It
was decided that stories involving Haugland could be submitted
at any time, but would be censored and held for release in the

order filed at a pre-determined time and date.

The first inkling I had of a problem was when Colonel B.A. Tormey, chief military censor, all six feet four inches of him, suddenly appeared at my desk and demanded gruffly:

"Hughes, who passed this story?"

A quick look at the files revealed that my stamp, No. 9, stood out boldly at the top of the typed sheet of paper.

I paled, but began my investigation under the colonel's baleful eye. I discovered that on the previous day one of the Haugland stories intended for "hold" had inadvertently been delivered by the Australian censor (without my knowledge) to the wireless room next door and was immediately transmitted to the U.S.

This Army Signal Corps photograph shows a group of war correspondents, along with two public relations officers, at 6th Army Headquarters at Milne Bay, New Guinea, just prior to a mission. Left to right, front row: Bill Wilson, UP; Edward Wallace, NBC; Frank Prist, Acme Newspictures; (naval officer unknown); Colonel Larry Lehrbas, PRO GHQ SWPA (who figures prominently in my article titled "MacArthur"); Frank Bagnall, Australian Department of Information; Norman Browns (same). Rear row: David Wittels, Philadelphia Record; Peter Hemery, Australian Broadcasting Commission; John Purcell, Life magazine; Major John Paarman, Australian PRO; Vern Haugland, AP (see "The Haugland Story"); Pen Raynor, Australian Evening Press; Frank Smith, Chicago Times; Hal O'Flaherty, Chicago News.

The worst aspect was that the story happened to be one filed by Don Caswell, of United Press, arch rival of Haugland's AP news service. Caswell had written a routine cover story of a couple of paragraphs. But the effect of the mix-up was to give UP a resounding scoop over AP on a major story involving an AP newsman.

AP staffers, of course, had written reams of copy about Haugland, but were still "beat" by more than 24 hours by the rival news service.

Talk about difficult to explain!

Yates McDaniel, AP bureau chief, had received urgent cables asking for an explanation. That's why Tormey stormed into my office.

At this stage, as a 27-year-old first lieutenant from Marietta, Georgia, I would have been quaking in my boots - if I had been wearing any.

After discovering I was the unwitting culprit, all Tormey said to me was, "Come on."

We went up one floor to the office of our boss, Colonel Legrande A. Diller, an aide to MacArthur. He greeted us perfunctorily with, "How's it going?"

My reply: "Colonel, all hell's broken loose."

After our explanation, all Diller said, with eyes blazing, was, "Come on."

The three of us, in grim silence, went up one more flight and marched to an office with an unmarked door. Diller went in immediately. Tormey and I waited just outside in an ante office where we overheard the entire conversation between Diller and MacArthur.

The colonel explained what had happened. Relief flooded my being as I heard MacArthur say: "Diller, we can't be overly concerned with these news service rivalries."

Now there was no one else who would say to me, "Come on."

As we were leaving MacArthur's office, all Diller did say was, "Hughes, keep better control of those stories."

And you can be sure I did, thereafter – for more than three years. As for Haugland, he left soon afterwards to join the Central

Pacific command press corps, and I never saw him again.

While on home leave in late 1944, I did receive a note from him expressing regret at having missed me when I passed through San Francisco, and congratulating me on a recent promotion. He was then in Honolulu, eventually bound for other combat areas.

Vern died in 1984, after choosing to live quietly in retirement in California for 11 years.

Following the war, I had seen his byline a number of times in local newspapers. As chief aviation writer for AP, he covered many splashdowns during the pioneer space-age programs. He also wrote a number of books on aviation and was considered a historian of some note on the subject.

In a eulogy to Vern, a friend and colleague of his wrote that "his modesty was painful, yet flecked with humor."

Here's how Vern was quoted as summing up his own achievements:

> (As a splashdown reporter), you go out on an aircraft carrier for two to six weeks at a time, cruise all around the warmer waters enjoying tanning sunshine, romantic moonlight nights on deck, Navy-type haute cuisine – and then watch heroic astronauts come floating down gracefully into the water.

> You maintain your standing – as the least expensive reporter who can be spared the longest time away from his regular job without being missed. You do this through the Mercury, Gemini and Apollo programs - and you automatically become the world's champion Wave Watcher, Maritime Freeloader and Flying-Fish Counter.

Among the tributes paid Haugland, this one by General Curtis E. LeMay, one-time Air Force Chief of Staff, best exemplified his status as a correspondent: "Of all the newsmen I've known, my friend Vern Haugland was the most trustworthy, accurate and objective."

Following his death, his ashes were sprinkled into the sea off San Clemente, California. His columnist-colleague wrote: "It seems as though my friend has just gone off on another assignment."

I wonder if by remote chance some of his ashes eventually washed against the verdant shores of New Guinea, where more than 59 years ago Vern Haugland so valiantly fought for survival – and won.

I celebrated my promotion to captain by having this picture taken, with two new bars gleaming, to send to my homefolks.

THE QUILL

A MAGAZINE FOR WRITERS, EDITORS, AND PUBLISHERS

SDX In the South Pacific. Three members of Sigma Delta Phi attached to General MacArthur's public relations staff are pictured above. Left to right, Capt. Edmund C. Hughes (Georgia '37); 1st Lieut. Charles J. Arnold (DePauw '40); and Capt. Harold B. Halter (Louisiana State '39).

The three persons pictured above are striking a pose simulating the photograph at left in which the same three appeared on the cover of *Quill*, the magazine of Sigma Delta Chi, national journalism fraternity, 41 years before at Port Moresby, New Guinea. The more recent photograph was taken at the reunion of General Diller's public relations staff in October 1985 at Bradenton, Florida. Since the war, Sigma Delta Chi's name has been changed to the Society of Professional Journalists, Sigma Delta Chi.

A WELCOME INTERLUDE OF HOME-LEAVE

In August of 1944, I was offered a 30-day leave of absence in the United States, exclusive of travel time. I readily accepted since I had been overseas almost two and a half years— which seemed an eternity.

Naturally, the long separation had brought about changes in my relationship with my wife, Frances, although she and I had corresponded faithfully and we still vowed in our letters mutual love and trust. By then, she had moved from Atlanta to Miami where she was living with her mother and our daughter, Corrie. She was still actively engaged in her singing career (for which I was glad) with the Opera Guild of Miami, having sung leading roles in some operatic productions there.

Corrie, now two, was pictured as a beautiful, curly-headed blonde, and I was most desirous of getting acquainted with her. Remember, she was only three weeks old when I left home.

I departed from Port Moresby, New Guinea, in mid August aboard a C-54 transport plane. Fellow passengers included comedian Jack Benny, movie star Carole Landis, singer Martha Tilton, and harmonica virtuoso Lew Adler, all of whom were touring combat areas to entertain troops. Benny looked and acted the part of a comedian, but, up close, Carole Landis was not nearly the glamorous beauty she portrayed on screen.

The entertainers left the plane at Guadalcanal, our first stop for refueling. The plane continued on to San Francisco, with four more refueling stops of approximately one hour each. We were in the air a total of some forty-eight hours.

The trip was extremely boring, as well as exhausting, mentally and physically, since time lost all meaning because we crossed so many different zones. But we could not say afterwards we suffered from "jet lag," as we were in a prop plane.

Arriving in San Francisco after a final brief stop in Hawaii, I immediately boarded a train for another long ride to Atlanta.

Atlanta had never looked better to me, and of course, I was overjoyed to see my family again. And, especially to be warmly greeted by Frances and Corrie. The joy was tempered somewhat when I learned that Frances was there only because of a fortuitous (for me) turn of events involving her singing career. I learned she had decided to leave Miami and had signed a contract with the Philadelphia Opera Company to sing leading roles while traveling over the U.S. But the contract was voided and the tour cancelled because of the shortage of male singers available due to the war. Otherwise, she would have been on the road with the opera company and unable to greet me in Atlanta.

In a twist of irony, the first role she had been scheduled to sing was Sonia, the lead in "The Merry Widow." All of this was soon erased from my mind by the sheer excitement of being at home. Various members of my birth family, including my mother and brother and sister, also displayed their pleasure at my return.

We were staying in Atlanta, but Frances and I visited friends in Marietta and were given a rousing reception. Part of this was due to the patriotic fervor enveloping the entire country. Otis Brumby was most cordial, and my impressions of the "new" Marietta were described in a byline story he asked me to write for the *Cobb County Times*.

Here's part of what I wrote in the story headlined "Major Ed Hughes Puts Stamp of Approval on Home Front":

"The main reason for this new, improved and more developed Marietta, I immediately realized, was the establishment and operation of the Bell bomber plant. While overseas, I had heard and read from time to time of the progress being made in construction of the enormous plant, how thousands of workmen were employed on the project, and how thousands of other persons, including many Mariettans, were being trained to mass-produce a 'Bell bomber' of unstated type. Then, one bright day in May there was flashed over the cable wires to Australia a story of how the new B-29 had bombed Japan a few days previously, and a feeling of elation and pride surged through me as I realized that many of the very same planes were produced in Marietta, my former home."

Upon visiting the bomber plant, I was struck by the physical size of the facility and, true to my journalistic training, attempted to describe my impressions:

"The plant itself, viewed from a distance, lent a false impression as to its size at first glance. Upon approaching closer, I realized this illusion was created by the fact that the plant dwarfs the smaller structures around it so completely that I was unconsciously comparing it with the surrounding hills and larger features of the landscape itself. However, this impression gave way to one of almost complete bewilderment when I began to comprehend the true magnitude of the place from a worm's eye view."

My story continued: "Then came the big thrill as I looked out on the apron of the runway and had my first close-up view of the Superfortress in all of its shining glory. Several of the giant machines were being warmed up for test flights. Busy mechanics swarmed over others, inspecting them to the last minute detail. Here was truly a breath-taking sight — one that certainly would have made the Japanese war lords quake in their down-at-the-heel boots."

"Following this brief look at the B-29, accompanied by my former boss, Otis Brumby, and my wife, I then had an enjoyable trip through the office section of the building where I encountered a number of old friends and associates I had known before entering the army."

Among those I mentioned "spending an enjoyable few minutes with" were: Jimmy Carmichael, vice-president of Bell Aircraft Corporation and general manager of the Marietta plant, Marietta Mayor Rip Blair, John Heck, Bill Sirmon, John Franklin, Emma Reeves Hewitt and Bill Kenney, former city editor of the *Times*.

The story ended with this paragraph: "To sum up my feelings about Marietta and Mariettans, it gave me a tremendous boost to see how the folks at home are supporting their men at war. Keep it up!"

CENSOR FOR MacARTHUR HOME, BUT WON'T TALK

BY PEGGY HUDGINS

"Interviewing a censor is a hard job, isn't it?" admitted Major Edmund C. Hughes, of Bolton, Ga., a member of General Douglas MacArthur's public relations staff at General Headquarters in Australia, who is home on leave and definitely not telling anything.

Major Hughes has spent more than two years with the General's staff in Australia and New Guinea and he lived next door to the General in Australia for a short time.

When advanced headquarters were moved to New Guinea, just before the New Britain campaign, Major Hughes followed the General there. His job was the censoring of all news released from the headquarters and all dispatches sent out by some 30 or 40 correspondents who have their own quarters in camp.

Says MacArthur Inspiring

Of General MacArthur he would say little, except that "to the men who work with him he is 'very

inspiring." At press conferences, he said, the General is a striking figure; he paces the floor as he talks, smoking cigars and scarcely pausing during the interview.

The General is rarely seen socially, he said, for he works very hard and spends his time in the office and his quarters. Major Hughes is proud of an autographed picture of the General which he sent home to his young daughter.

Met McLemore

Major Hughes told of meeting Henry McLemore in Australia and he said that the correspondent is as witty and humorous in his speech as in his writings. Raymond Clapper he met too, just three days before Clapper was killed.

News from the correspondents, Major Hughes said, can be relayed from New Guinea by beam wireless to San Francisco in 10 minutes and that within a very short time after a press conference is

over, the dispatches are in San Francisco.

When asked if he had any Japanese "souvenirs," Major Hughes produced his collection of Japanese money, called "invasion money," by the Yanks. It was printed by the Japs at the beginning of the war, in anticipation of Japanese occupation of Australia and Pacific islands and there are Australian pound notes, Dutch guilder notes and even shilling notes. The money, of course, had no real value, but he said that the Japs planned to force it upon people of "occupied" countries as currency exchange.

His impressions of Australia are mostly of the friendliness of the people, "the Aussies are real Allies", and amusement at the language, some of which he picked up after his long stay there. The girls of Australia, he said, are picking up American customs from the Yank doughboys, and have adopted jitterbugging with enthusiasm.

He met Mrs. Roosevelt when she came to Australia and on his trip home, he flew with Jack Benny, Carole Landis and Lew Adler, who had just finished an entertainment tour. He didn't get

to talk much to Benny, however, because all the people on the plane kept the comedian busy signing short-snorter bills.

Major Hughes, formerly editor of the Cobb County Times, Marietta, Ga., is the son of Mrs. M. A. Hughes, of Bolton. His wife is the former Miss Frances Campbell, of Cleveland, Tenn.

Frances and I also traveled south, spending a long weekend at the Cloister on Sea Island.

From the beginning of my home stay, Corrie and I spent much time together, and soon she was acting just like any two-year-old with her daddy.

Although far from feeling like a celebrity, I was complimented when an *Atlanta Journal* reporter called and asked to interview me for a feature story. Despite my considerable experience in dealing with war correspondents, I had misgivings about doing the interview, since some misinterpretation of what I said could have resulted in problems for me. I also was wary of being misquoted. But, fortunately, the reporter was competent and the interview went smoothly. The story is at left.

Finally, the day of departure came. Good-byes were said, and I began the arduous return trip. I landed at Hollandia, New Guinea, in early October and resumed my PR duties amid frantic preparation by my colleagues to leave for the invasion of the Philippines. But I had returned too late to be included, it was decided, and I was left in charge of our small PR contingent at Hollandia.

A few weeks after my return, a letter from Frances informed me that she was expecting our second child. I was enormously pleased, of course, and this time hoped for a son. That hope was fulfilled on May 27 when a healthy baby boy was delivered by Frances at an Atlanta hospital. He was named by his mother, Edmund Jackson. The name Jackson was for an uncle of Frances', E. Jack Smith, her mother's brother.

My son was five months old before I first saw him. So I missed some of the diaper stages of both children's lives.

AN EVENING WITH IRVING BERLIN

Was Irving Berlin a fraud? Were some of his songs suspect as to who composed them?

I read with more than casual interest in a recent issue of Parade magazine a question and answer column item questioning the integrity of the legendary composer.

The questioner stated that some senior citizens in his group claim the late Irving Berlin did not compose all the music and lyrics for the songs which bear his name, adding:

"Throughout his life, it has been alleged, aspiring songwriters approached Berlin with musical compositions, for which they were paid a small sum and for which they signed over all rights to him. What's the real truth?"

The answer: "'The real truth' is there is no truth to that old fairy tale. Irving Berlin, who died in 1989 at age 101, was a great and prolific composer-lyricist in his own right."

Add a fervent amen to that answer, based on what I learned in a conversation I had with Irving Berlin nearly 57 years ago.

For some years past, with news media recording each recurring birthday of Irving Berlin, my mind would flash back to a remote coastal village in the verdant, tangled wildland of New Guinea, just a few degrees below the equator. It was at Hollandia (now known as Jayapura) that I spent a memorable evening with the noted composer.

I was at Hollandia in the U.S. Army as a public relations officer on the staff of General Douglas MacArthur. Here we were a rear echelon unit of MacArthur's headquarters. The main group had pulled out a few weeks earlier for the invasion of the Philippines. I would have participated in that, but I had returned from home leave too late to be included, and was left temporarily in charge of this small encampment.

My earliest recollection of Irving Berlin and his music stems from childhood, when my older sister would play his songs at the piano and I would join her in singing them.

What impressed me even then was that the sheet music read "Words and Music by Irving Berlin" rather than naming separate lyricist and composer as did virtually every other piece of sheet music of the day.

In my youthful mind was this thought: What genius it must take to produce both words and music for such outstanding songs.

One recent evening as I sat fascinated by the PBS telecast of "Great Performances: Irving Berlin's America," I was struck again by the beauty and range of his works. And how prolific he was — with nearly 1,000 songs to his credit, including such standards as "Alexander's Ragtime Band," "God Bless America," "White Christmas," and a host of others.

The telecast recaptured memories of that evening more than half a century ago.

It was Christmas Eve, 1944.

"Major, there's a fellow out here says he's Irving Berlin."

"Show him in, sergeant."

Because of the afternoon tropical heat, I stood in my tent, clad in a pair of underwear shorts, preparatory to dressing for dinner.

There was no mistaking the identity of the person the sergeant led into my tent. It was Irving Berlin! — at that time, the best known composer in the world of popular music.

His slight, upright figure was clothed in the same khaki uniform with open collar that we wore, but with no insignia of any kind. Despite his casual attire, with a shock of neatly-combed jet black hair topping his small stature, he presented a natty overall appearance. His dark eyes, under bushy eyebrows, darted impatiently between me and the sergeant.

Explaining that he was in New Guinea to put on a production of his show, "This Is the Army," Berlin said that Lanny Ross, a well known former radio network singer, then a first lieutenant with Army Special Services, was to have met him at the airfield, and had failed to appear. He asked if we could put him up for the night.

We were delighted to do so, assigning him to an empty tent.

After showering, the composer returned to my tent for a couple of drinks, and the beginning of a memorable evening.

For more than two hours, we chatted casually and easily, mostly about his career as a song writer, and some of his experiences as a giant figure in show business during several decades.

The talk centered on his composing, and how he created such catchy lyrics and tuneful melodies.

"The best way I can describe it, it's a sort of stream-of-consciousness method. Ideas come to mind and I sift them out and try to blend the words and music into an acceptable song. Not all are acceptable, however, by any means."

Impressed as I was, both by his stature as a celebrity and his charming personality, I still had the audacity to bring out of my footlocker the sheet music of an unpublished song for which I had written the lyrics.

To my surprise, he refused even to glance at the sheet of music, and would not discuss it further. His reason: he could not afford to listen to or look at any type of original music because he could easily become the target of a plagiarism suit in connection with music he might publish in the future.

He chuckled over the fact that I had dug out the song to show him.

"It happens to me all the time, " he exclaimed.

When I inquired as to how he began his career as a composer, he replied:

"I arrived in the United States at the age of four as a member of a Russian immigrant's family. After my father died, I left school at 14 and became a street singer in New York City. This led to being a singing waiter at a beer hall. Once you start singing, you start thinking about writing your own songs."

He said he composed at the piano.

"I'm not able to transpose from one key to another, so I have a specially built piano that can transpose songs with the twist of a lever. I bought the piano — which I still use — in 1909 for $100. I play — and compose — only in F sharp major, or just on the black keys. Also, I can't read music."

Volleyball at Hollandia, with rugged mountains in background.

At Hollandia, center tent, the very place where I entertained Irving Berlin.

What an anomaly, I thought, to have written so many great songs, without being able to read music!

Meanwhile, Lanny Ross called, apologizing for the mix-up at the airfield, and offered to come over and pick up Irving Berlin and return him to Lanny's encampment.

Berlin refused, saying, "I will stay here with Major Hughes."

That evening a Christmas party in our nearby mess hall, attended by the 25 or 30 people assigned to my outfit, came off as scheduled, with our distinguished visitor as guest of honor. We invited Lanny to join us, which he did.

The entire affair was a tribute to Irving Berlin and his music.

All the party-goers knew the words to most of his songs, and the highlight of the evening was group singing of "White Christmas" to his piano accompaniment.

During the merriment, a Signal Corps photographer took many pictures to record the evening for us. Unfortunately, all the photographs were somehow misplaced and lost in a household move several years after the war.

The next morning, upon leaving, Mr. Berlin thanked me for our hospitality, and presented me with a parting gift of a bottle of Old Overholt Rye Whiskey.

A belated toast to the memory of Irving Berlin!

If the person who recently wrote to Parade Magazine questioning his integrity had met and talked with Irving Berlin as I did, odds are the letter never would have been written.

New Guinea Memories —Pictorially

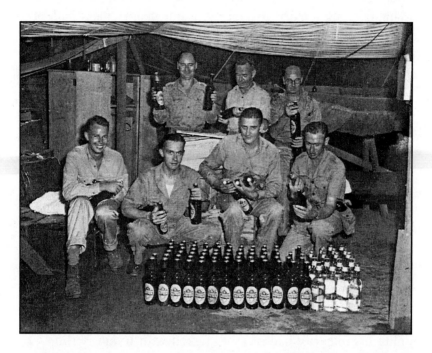

New Guinea was dry — and I don't mean the climate. Above gag photo was staged after a rare air shipment of Australian booze arrived at Hollandia. Colleague Dick Brewer is seated at left, and I'm second from right, with unknown officer between us. The others are Aussies.

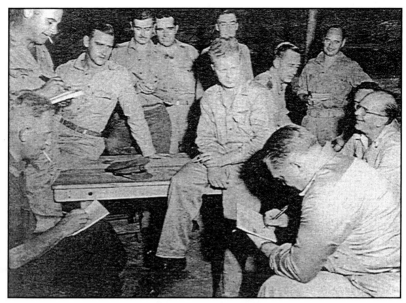

With the heading "Sky Talk by Ace of Aces," this photograph appeared in newspapers throughout the U.S. in 1944. One caption read: "A natural in the clouds or before a battery of reporters, Major Richard Bong (center, seated on table) kingpin of U.S. aces with 27 'kills' is interviewed by members of the allied press in New Guinea." I am at left with my hand on table. Bong was good at poker, too, I learned.

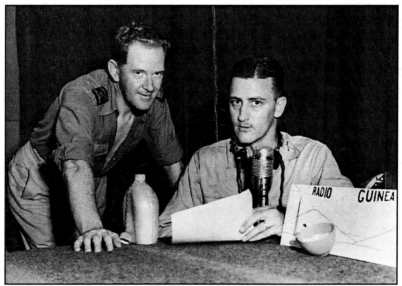

Broadcasting "live" from New Guinea to U.S. over NBC Blue Network New Year's Eve, 1943. At left is Australian correspondent also on the program.

DRAMA IN MANILA

A ir traffic was slack at Nichols Field in Manila that day. Few sounds marred the quietness except for the desultory drone of an occasional airplane in the distance. Suddenly, just after 10 a.m., a lone four-engined U.S. Air Force transport plane knifed through the heavy cloud cover and glided to a smooth landing on the grease-stained concrete runway.

The date: August 19, 1945.

Close up, 100 or so military personnel witnessed the landing. These were mostly members of General MacArthur's staff, including 10 of us in public relations, plus 75 to 80 war correspondents. Several hundred curious U.S. servicemen were roped off from the immediate viewing area.

What distinguished this plane from others was its passengers. They were Japanese, 16 of them, arriving in the capital city of the Philippines while the war technically was still in progress, although a cease-fire was in effect.

Five days earlier the Japanese government, through Emperor Hirohito's dramatic radio broadcast, had made its offer to surrender. Carrying out a directive from MacArthur, this arriving delegation had been dispatched from Japan in two Japanese planes, painted white and marked with green crosses. The two planes rendezvoused on a small island with our Air Force plane. The Japanese then transferred to it and were flown to Manila.

The purpose of the trip was for the Japanese to receive instructions from MacArthur and for them to provide him with the necessary mass of information for the forthcoming surrender of Japan and the beginning of its occupation.

All eyes were riveted on the cargo door as the Japanese came down the ramp from the plane. They were an ill-assorted group, grim-faced and sullen, about half of them in uniform and the rest in civilian clothes.

Foremost in the greeting party was U.S. Colonel Sidney F. Mashbir, an expert on Japanese affairs and fluent in the language, who was to serve as interpreter and adviser for us throughout the protracted proceedings. As Colonel Mashbir advanced towards the plane, the ranking Japanese officer — a lieutenant general — offered to shake hands with him. Colonel Mashbir instinctively raised his hand, and then suddenly withdrew it, apparently realizing that protocol decreed he not do so; they were to be treated as conquered enemies and not shown any courtesies such as a handshake or salute.

As Japanese envoys leave plane at Manila, Colonel Mashbir salutes their U.S. escorting officer.

The incident survives in print. In my files is a news magazine with a photograph of Colonel Mashbir, with right hand partially extended, and perplexity clearly written on his face.

As a military censor, my assignment was to accompany Merrill Mueller of NBC to within a few feet of the Japanese delegation in order to censor a "live" broadcast Mueller was making to the U.S., under a pool arrangement, over all four major networks.

Censoring of a broadcast being made in this manner — ad libbed "live" without a pre-censored script — was unprecedented. To my knowledge, never had wartime censorship been in operation while a broadcast was actually in progress.

During the broadcast, which was being picked up and monitored in Japan, an incident occurred in which I felt almost compelled to jerk the microphone from Mueller's hands, cutting him off the air. He was describing the appearance of the Japanese as they descended from the big C-54. He said:

"Their uniforms are of a dirty, green color. They are very ugly... in fact, they are hideous."

I quickly tugged at his arm and put a finger to my lips. He said nothing further in that vein, and the remainder of the broadcast went smoothly.

It was an especially tense moment in history. There was no certainty the Japanese would not renege on their offer to surrender. Any nation is proud of its uniform; thus what Mueller said could have been construed as an insult, thereby causing a possible breakdown in the surrender arrangements.

Later, over a drink, Mueller and I discussed the incident, and he acknowledged he had gone too far, but the possible consequences still weighed heavily on my censorial mind.

Merrill Mueller of NBC.

My colleagues of two or more years photographed in Manila on June 1, 1945. Back row (l. to r.): Captain Selwyn Pepper, (myself), Captain Frederick Λ. German, Captain John L. Cross, Jr., Captain Charles J. Arnold. Front row (l. to r.): Major Norman H. Myers, Lieutenant Colonel P.F. LaFollette (executive officer and former three-term governor of Wisconsin), Brigadier General L.A. Diller (chief public relations officer), and Major Jerry Baulch (my closest friend and roommate for awhile at the Carlton Hotel in Brisbane).

A Filipino and I survey downtown Manila's almost total devastation.

13
BORNEO INVASION

In recording these reminiscences, one experience above all others deserves an asterisk. That occurred during the invasion of Borneo when I was pinned down by enemy mortar fire in a shell crater next to one occupied by the chosen successor to Ernie Pyle — Frank Miller, of Scripps-Howard newspapers. Miller had newly arrived in our area to carry on the tradition of the GI Joe personal reporting style made famous by Pyle.

Pyle, who in 1943 won the Pulitizer Prize for distinguished war correspondence, was killed April 18, 1945 by Japanese gunfire on the tiny island of Ie Shima while observing the U.S. landing on nearby Okinawa. Pyle was making his way to MacArthur's command in Manila where, undoubtedly, I would have known him and censored some of his stories.

The invasion of Tarakan Island, just off Borneo, began only 12 days after Pyle's untimely death. My job, along with two colleagues, was to escort a handful of 15 or so correspondents during the invasion and censor what they wrote.

After flying from Manila to Moroti, a small Indonesian island just south of the Philippine archipelago, which served as a staging area for the operation, we boarded an LCI (Landing Craft Infantry) and set sail for Borneo. Our convoy included a wide assortment of ships, ranging from PT boats to heavy cruisers.

At first, it was almost a pleasure cruise. We had idyllic weather for several days. Everyone was in a jovial mood. There were even rumors of booze being aboard in some quarters (strictly taboo on a combat ship during a mission), but these were never confirmed — although on occasion I did observe a correspondent or two listing and bobbing on deck a little more than would have been warranted by the ship's pitch and roll.

The Borneo invasion, except for softening up of the several landing sites and close support by a U.S. naval task force, was primarily an Australian show. Aussie ground forces making the landing were elements of the Ninth "Rats of Torbruck" Division, famous for its unsurpassed fighting record in the Middle East and Africa.

Although Miller and I went ashore via different routes, we ended up in adjacent shell craters after coming under heavy mortar fire. The shell craters resulted from the bombardment by our naval guns.

Leaving our LCI, Miller and three other correspondents had transferred to a PT boat and were transported to a heavily damaged dock. There, to reach shore, they were forced to crawl along a slippery oil pipeline while under enemy shelling and machine gun fire.

After returning to the LCI, a relatively small ship with twin ramps on either side of the bow, Frank Miller secluded himself and pecked out his story on the traditional so-called "battered" typewriter.

Stories were written in tight language called "cableleses." This means that words were shortened, run together, and sometimes distorted — all in the interest of economy since charges for transmission were based on the number of words, no matter how bunched up and unintelligible they were. This resulted in a sort of code, compounding the woes of the hapless censor.

Nevertheless, I happened to save the thin, now crinkled with age, carbon copy of Miller's story — with typed strike-throughs for deletions and neatly penciled-in additions - just as he submitted it to me for censorship. The first sheet, one of three, bears the imprint of my stamp in bright red ink, reading "Passed Military Censor GHQ (General Headquarters) 9 (my individual number) S.W.P.A. (Southwest Pacific Area)." Here's the beginning of that story, exactly as written by Miller, with my own interpretation of certain words and phrases in parentheses for clarification:

via press wireless
scrippshoward ward washington
exmiller (from Miller) aboard an ell cee eye (LCI) off
tarakan comma May first if anybodyd (anybody had)

told me six months ago eyed (I would) be setting foot on
soil of borneo today eyed (I would) have thought him
daffy para (paragraph) smorning (this morning) eye (I)
set not only foot but elbows knees and torso stop

Miller went on to describe how he "watched our warships pitch
in shells and rockets" and saw "Aussie beetwentyfours (B-24's)
lay beautifully accurate strings of bombs along the left flank of
our landings. We had seen first wave of amphtracks creep into
smoking shore and disgorge digger (Australian) troops with no
apparent opposition."

"Columns of smoke and large fires were visible. Offshore area
was dotted with warships, assault transports and small craft."

Our landing was less spectacular than Miller's as the rest of us
aboard the LCI had come ashore in more conventional fashion
with the ship lowering its ramps for us to emerge — even though
we did experience some welcome wetness from the warm waters of the Celebese Sea.

The dull thump of Japanese mortar fire had no counterpart in
my limited experience. I had been shot at by Japanese snipers in
the Philippines while traversing the plains of central Luzon on
the drive to Manila. The distinctive whine of those bullets just
overhead I clearly remembered.

This was different, and more scary.

I wanted to burrow deeper into the terra firma, like some des-
perate animal. Yet, there were no tools for doing so. It was a
helpless feeling as the shelling became more and more intense.
Mortar shells popped up all around us — some quite close. Conversations between shell holes were at a minimum, limited mostly
to deep grunts and muted profanities. As for my part, the experience put new meaning in the cliché, "There are no atheists in
foxholes."

After about an hour, the shelling gradually subsided and we
climbed out, sore and somewhat shaken, and made it back to the
ship. As we climbed aboard the LCI, it was like returning home
after a long and tiring journey.

Miller had ended his message in this way (which happened to
coincide with my feelings exactly):

"... we all eventually got back aboard this vessel, bruised a little and some of us greenstained from the flora of Borneo. It was my first landing. And that'll be enough for this week."

Receiving a Bronze Star medal for my limited part in the action was extremely anti-climatic and unexpected.

As a footnote: Just after our return to Manila, Miller engaged in some controversy with his employer. In an exchange of cablegrams, during which Miller resigned, his editor asked that he reconsider and stay on.

Here's how Miller succinctly answered in a classic five-word cablegram which I happened to censor:

"You heard me I quit"

That, also, deserves an asterisk — in my book.

CITATION FOR BRONZE STAR MEDAL

Major Edmund C. Hughes, O353558, Infantry, Army of the United States. For meritorious achievement in connection with military operations against the enemy in the Southwest Pacific Area from 5 July 1942 to 17 May 1945. As an Assistant Public Relations Officer of the Public Relations Office, General Headquarters, Southwest Pacific Area, he served in New Guinea and the Philippine Islands. In the Tarakan operation he acted as one of the conducting officers. Major Hughes, through his wide knowledge of news coverage, enthusiasm, and intelligence, was responsible in a high degree for the excellent news coverage of the operations in which he participated. His loyal, efficient service and devotion to duty contributed in a large degree to the success of public relations activities in the Southwest Pacific Area.

Home address: Mrs. Frances C. Hughes (wife),
              c/o Mrs. M. A. Hughes,
              Bolton, Ga.

Author immediately after
Borneo action.

Receiving congratulations from General Diller after presenting me with the
Bronze Star medal following the Borneo operation.

FINAL DESTINATION: TOKYO

It was the last leg on the road to Tokyo.

There was an atmosphere of tense quiet among the 24 passengers of the big, plush C-54 transport plane awaiting take-off in the early morning of August 30, 1945. Following the six-hour flight from Manila two days earlier, we were at Okinawa. It was just prior to our leaving for the initial occupation of Japan, as a prelude to the surrender ceremony.

Typhoons raging in the Western Pacific between Okinawa and Japan had delayed by 48 hours the timetable for beginning the occupation. It was as though through the violent storms, the gods were purging the seas of the blood lost in the four-year carnage by both Allied and Japanese fighting men.

Originally scheduled for August 31, the surrender ceremony was now set for September 2. This had resulted in a two-day stop-over for us at Okinawa.

Conversations were hushed in the dimly lit cabin of the plane, but excitement was heightened by a spirit of adventure we felt at being among the first to go into the heart of the enemy's country even before they were disarmed.

Later General MacArthur described the initial occupation as one of the greatest gambles in history, and added:

"Our ground forces were outnumbered a thousand to one but the stakes were worth it."

Before boarding, I was handed a passenger list and informed that I was to be the plane captain. As such, I was responsible for all passengers, including 18 war correspondents, two other officers and three enlisted men. Heading the list was Brigadier General LeGrande A. Diller, MacArthur's public relations chief and my boss since beginning the long trek from Melbourne, Australia. Diller, who was affectionately called "Pick," was one of the 14 officers MacArthur chose to accompany him in his dramatic escape from the Philippines in at PT boat in early 1942.

The other officer was Lieutenant Colonel Richard Powell, a former Philadelphia newspaperman, who became a successful author following the war. One of his books was made into a motion picture starring Jimmy Stewart.

Among the correspondents was Bill Dunn, whose voice had become familiar to CBS listeners as he broadcast throughout the Southwest Pacific war. Bill, with his considerable girth, was pictured in news photos with MacArthur sloshing ashore during the Leyte landing.

Incidentally, both General Diller and Bill Dunn were featured prominently as commentators in several episodes of the widely-acclaimed 1985 telecast of "American Caesar," based on William Mansfield's well balanced biography of MacArthur.

Then, too, there was Merrill Mueller of NBC whose "live" broadcast I had censored while he described the arrival of the Japanese emissaries in Manila on August 19.

Also on board were several news service men including Don Caswell of UP and Russell Brines and Ralph Teatsworth, both of AP, all of whom I had worked with closely during my escorting and censoring chores.

Ours was the first of five similar planes carrying early 100 print newsmen and broadcasters in one of the largest mass flights of correspondents of the war.

The huge aircraft shuddered perceptibly as its four engines roared to full throttle, their propellers biting into the night air, preparatory to takeoff. We were airborne at 2:15 a.m. and landed at Atsugi airstrip near Tokyo at 7:25 a.m.

The flight was uneventful, except for one small incident. While flying over the southern islands approaching Japan, several puffs of gray smoke, accompanied by sounds of muffled explosions, suddenly appeared at the windows of our plane, seemingly just a short distance away. The burst looked like balls of fluffy cotton candy that one could almost reach out and touch. It was unmistakably anti-aircraft fire from the ground.

"Looks like somebody didn't get the word," one correspondent dryly remarked.

Were we flying into some huge ambush? The Japanese were well known for their treachery. Would we be among the victims if this happened? Such thoughts were soon dismissed as I settled back in my comfortable seat to savor the prospects of going home after nearly three and a half years — if the occupation went well.

GENERAL MACARTHUR AT ATSUGI

With his corncob pipe jutting rakishly from his firmly set jaw, General of the Army Douglas MacArthur paused on the second step of the ramp from his plane *Bataan* and gazed over the scene with obvious satisfaction.

The silhouette of MacArthur and his pipe against the patchy blue sky over Atsugi airfield remains etched in my memory as vividly as any other picture from my wartime experiences.

After his short pause, he came down the ramp to join the surging group of reporters, photographers and servicemen — all eager for a close-up glimpse of the five-star general who was soon to become the first foreigner in 2,600 years to take over custody of Japan.

MacArthur was almost jaunty in manner, appearing more relaxed and at ease than on the other occasions I had observed him during the Southwest Pacific war. All previous times, as during one of his first press conferences after arriving in Melbourne in mid-1942, he was tense and brooding. This was just after he made his famous declaration, "I shall return," bolstering the hopes and morale of the Philippine people.

Here's how one news magazine described him and the scene:

"Usually strained and austere, that day at Atsugi the general seemed calm and happy as he puffed his pipe. He called first names, clasped hands and complimented the military band, saying 'that's about the sweetest music I've ever heard.'

"As photographers crowded close for pictures, MacArthur posed patiently. He even turned so a Japanese photographer could take his picture."

MacArthur arrived at mid-afternoon, August 30, just eight hours after the first airborne troops had secured the airfield.

Three majors at final destination: Atsugi Airdrome.
Left to right: Me, Gordon Sinykin and Jerry Baulch.

The occupation began in force the day before as 11th Airborne troops dropped down on Atsugi while simultaneously British and American marines went ashore at the Yokosuka navy yard.

One correspondent reported: "This was the last beachhead and they hit it standing up."

Meanwhile, U.S. and British warships advanced through the channel into Tokyo Bay. Overhead roared hundreds of carrier-based planes providing a vast umbrella of protective cover.

As the occupation proceeded, B-29s carrying troops came down at four minute intervals, and we watched as they quickly unloaded and took off.

Our C-54 with the 18 correspondents aboard was the 21st plane of more than 200 to land at Atsugi that day.

Since our early morning arrival, we in public relations had engaged continuously in censoring the steady stream of news stories being written by the 100 or so correspondents on hand. This writing was mostly about what we were witnessing just after it happened. Or, in some cases, even as it was happening.

One strange sight I remember well was the hundreds of dilapidated American-made Japanese cars surrounding the airfield. This was in accordance with MacArthur's pre-occupation instructions to provide transportation for us. The cars, some of which used charcoal for fuel, were extremely old and most were difficult to start. It was not unusual to see two or three uniformed Americans, sometimes helped by a Japanese, frantically pushing a beat-up vehicle, to no avail.

It was in one such vehicle — a 1932 vintage Packard sedan, as I recall — that I traveled the 20 miles to Yokohama.

Along the way, we rode through pretty countryside, seemingly undamaged by war. We learned later that the Japanese had chosen to guide us through areas least ravaged by bombs.

Armed Japanese guards stood with backs turned towards us at intervals all along the route to Yokohama. Interpreters explained to us that the turning of backs was their way of showing the utmost respect for us as conquerors. They did the same in the presence of the emperor. People standing in doorways turned their faces away from us as we drove past.

Yokohama was almost completely destroyed by U.S. bombs. Only the picturesque waterfront area had been spared.

The New Grand Hotel, situated on the waterfront, had been taken over as MacArthur's headquarters. The hotel, built of concrete and said to be earthquake proof, was described in pre-war tourist folders as comparing favorably with American hotels.

Not unexpectedly, it was not my privilege to stay in one of the hotel's 120 rooms.

Instead, we in public relations were assigned temporary bil-lets in a much less imposing hotel, a few blocks away, featuring a menu of mostly inedible food and with a fish smell permeating the air.

That night, never had K-rations tasted so much like *haute cuisine.*

PR officers and correspondents celebrate our arrival at Atsugi.
I'm second from left.

HERO AND TRAITOR AT YOKOHAMA

16

At Yokohama, just preceding and following the surrender ceremony, I encountered on separate occasions two people, both prominent in the news, who were as diverse as could be imagined.

One was a man, the other a woman.

One was American, the other Japanese.

One was a hero, the other a traitor.

One was General Jonathan "Skinny" Wainwright, the other Tokyo Rose.

General Wainwright had been rescued by parachutists a few days earlier from a Japanese prison camp in Manchuria after three years and three months of captivity. Wainwright was the commander at Corregidor whom General MacArthur was forced to leave behind in early 1942 when he was ordered to Australia by President Roosevelt. Wainwright struggled to hold the island fortress, but the odds were overwhelming against him as he waited in vain for promised reinforcements and resupply.

Wainwright, just turned 62, was acclaimed a hero after release from his long imprisonment. Congratulatory messages came flooding in from leaders throughout the free world. He later revealed to MacArthur that he had fully expected to be in disgrace and court-martialed for his surrender at Corregidor.

His voice reportedly shook as he said during an interview:

"I have had little contact with the outside world, but I... believe the War Department and the American people have accepted my dire disaster with a forbearance and a generosity greater than any in the experience of any other defeated commander... "

At Yokohama, he was embraced by his old commander, General MacArthur, and sat down to dinner served by bowing Japanese. There was a pistol at his hip.

To U.S. correspondents, Wainwright said: "It's good to be back a free man and an American wearing a gun again."

The setting was the dining room of the New Grand Hotel, MacArthur's temporary headquarters, where correspondents were waiting to interview him.

During a slight lull, he was seated alone at a small table in an alcove adjoining the dining room. As I approached him, he stood up and we shook hands. I congratulated him upon his release. He appeared very thin but in good spirits. He was gaunt, and his voice weak.

On September 2, he was at MacArthur's side to witness the formal surrender ceremony aboard the battleship Missouri, and was presented the first of five pens with which MacArthur signed the document.

Then, as a fitting climax, he journeyed to Baguio to accept the surrender of all Japanese in the Philippines from the now declawed "Tiger of Malaya," Lieutenant General Tomoyuki Yamashita.

Yamashita was later executed as a war criminal.

As for Tokyo Rose, she was brought in by two war correspondents at Yokohama and was immediately taken into custody for questioning.

Tokyo Rose, siren of the Pacific, became a legend among servicemen for the taunting, provocative remarks she made during her propaganda broadcasts throughout the war.

I heard her many times as did thousands of soldiers, sailors, airmen, and marines as her lilting, beguiling voice came crackling over the air waves. In intermittent bursts of sound, her words and recorded popular music were beamed to us from a powerful short wave radio transmitter in Tokyo.

As patently obvious as it was that the broadcasts were propaganda, it's extremely doubtful that she ever adversely affected the morale of servicemen as was intended.

Many a GI or sailor on a lonely evening watch chuckled as he heard her dulcet tones, often with sensual overtones. She called names, supposedly of wives and girlfriends, made innuendos casting doubt as to their morality and questioning their faithfulness, all meant to create discontent and unrest in the minds of her listeners.

Nightly she bombarded the marines at Guadalcanal during the fiercest fighting there with her propaganda barbs. At times, she even predicted troop movements, naming the outfits involved, and saying when and where a particular attack would take place. Usually she was wrong, but occasionally, to our consternation, she would be correct. Obviously, her information was based on Japanese intelligence reports.

There was much speculation among servicemen about her looks, but all such fantasies were in a jocular vein. Was she a dark beauty like Heddy Lamar? Or more in the mold of blond Betty Grable, the pinup favorite of the time?

"When we get to Tokyo we'll look up Tokyo Rose for a date," was a remark often heard.

It was September 4, two days after the surrender ceremony. I happened to be in a building taken over for temporary working space when Tokyo Rose was brought into an adjoining office for questioning.

Her looks belied her sultry voice.

With dark eyes and straggly straight hair, with bangs, she made no pretense to stylishness. A prominent nose protruded sharply from her round face, which was devoid of makeup.

Her husband stood just outside the office door and waited patiently during the interrogation. He was a swarthy Portuguese of small stature, with spaniel eyes, and appeared sullen and ill at ease.

Later in the day, we held a full-scale press conference for correspondents, and I learned more about Tokyo Rose.

Born Iva Ikuki Toguri, she was an American nisei graduate of UCLA. She claimed she happened to be visiting in Japan when the war started and was forced to remain. While held a captive, she said she was coerced into making the broadcasts.

Tried under her married name, D'Aquino, she was convicted of treason in 1949 and imprisoned until 1956. She steadfastly claimed to have worked under duress. On January 19, 1977 President Gerald Ford granted her a pardon.

General Wainwright died in 1953 and was buried with all the honors befitting his status as a military hero.

Today, based on sketchy news reports, Tokyo Rose lives quietly somewhere in the Midwest. Wonder how often she recalls her days as a glorified disc jockey serving the war lords of Japan. Perhaps, now only she knows the truth as to whether she willingly served or not.

17

TOKYO EXCURSION

Tokyo had seemed an almost mythical place since we started out from Melbourne, Australia, nearly three and a half years earlier. After Melbourne came Brisbane... then Townsville... Sydney... Port Moresby... Hollandia... Leyte... Manila... Borneo... Okinawa — all stops along the road to Tokyo.

We went into the Japanese capital August 31, 1945, two days before the surrender ceremony.

A letter I wrote to my former employer, a weekly newspaper publisher, described the trip in detail:

> I entered Tokyo today under weird circumstances, and virtually alone. There was no comforting sight of GIs standing guard at street intersections as at Yokohama which I had seen occupied by 11th Airborne troops the previous day.
>
> In Tokyo I felt alone — alone with one other public relations officer and 16 war correspondents. We were alone in the enemy capital, which had a pre-war population of six million people, two days before any surrender documents were scheduled to be signed. I don't mean for this to sound like I was a hero of any sort. I wasn't. In fact, I probably would have been downright scared if the experience had not been so engrossing.
>
> The trip, entire unplanned, resulted from a casual remark by a captain-friend of mine while we were having breakfast at Yokohama this morning. He said, simply: "Let's go to Tokyo."
>
> We knew a couple of correspondents had gone into the city the previous afternoon, but apart from that no other Americans had been there, to our knowledge. We found a correspondent who had commandeered a Japanese truck and induced him to drive. But the word spread that we

were going and 15 other correspondents piled into the uncovered body of the truck. All were eager to go, despite the steady rain.

No one knew which road to take, but we were aided in getting out of Yokohama by a sign in English pointing towards Tokyo. This, incidentally, was the only English road sign we saw. We were also helped some by following the general direction of an electric train line running between the two cities.

Along the entire route stand the factories and industrial plants in which Japan forged the implements of war employed in a vain effort to conquer the world. Today these places are strangely quiet.

It was impossible to obtain directions from civilians. Those who didn't appear too scared to answer our queries were unable to understand English. Some even ran when we stopped to question them. Many had the look of a frightened animal when accosted.

Women would peek from behind window coverings as we passed, while men would stare from a safe distance whenever they thought we were not looking at them. A little child would tug at his mother's clothing to attract her attention to us. I saw one woman rush back into her house to call other members of her family to come look. For virtually all of them, we were the first Americans they had seen in nearly four years. And for some, we were the first Americans they had ever seen.

The looks they gave us ranged from mildly curious to openly belligerent. But looks of fear and surprise were the most numerous. Some appeared to be dazed. They had heard their Emperor say that the war was over and the Americans would occupy their country, but either they had not expected it so soon or else they were deeply shocked by the reality of it after long years of such personal sacrifice and suffering.

There was no smiling or waving of hands, except occasionally by very small children who simply did not understand what our presence signified.

As we rode through this now deathly silent industrial area, I had the feeling that these people had absolutely no sense of guilt. It appeared they felt simply that they had lost the war, but only as one loses in a poker game or some other game of chance. They had gambled for high stakes, but the cards were against them. Now, one of the penalties for losing was to put up with their country being occupied by a race of people called Americans — their enemies. And they were putting up with it only because their Emperor had ordered them to do so.

Tokyo was almost a ghost city. This effect was heightened by the utter devastation we saw block after block. Certain areas were completely obliterated without even any rubble of the destroyed houses and buildings remaining. In some sections makeshift shanties had been erected over the ruins to provide living quarters. One of the most striking features of this picture of ruin was that there were no bomb craters. It was obvious that the new fire bomb had been at work here. It appeared as though some giant flame thrower had been used to spurt its tongues in all directions. In some large areas not a single object was left standing. Not a wall, a tree, or even a post was upright as a result of our incendiary bombing attacks. One correspondent remarked: "Wouldn't it warm the hearts of those B-29 boys if they could see this?" And I believe it would have. The destruction wrought by the Japanese I saw in Manila was terrific, but this was worse.

Although the streets were not deserted, the city certainly did not contain anywhere near its pre-war population. One informed observer estimated that only about two million of the original six million inhabitants remain. The emptiness of the streets, added to the other weird aspects of our visit, made us feel even less comfortable. But apart from a few defiant stares, we saw no evidence of open hostility. It appeared to be something of a "cat and mouse" game with the Japanese adopting an attitude of watchful waiting to determine how we as victors would treat them. I was riding in the front seat with the captain and the correspondent-driver (who happened to be Charles Rawlings, of the *Saturday Evening Post*, the husband of Marjorie Kinnan Rawlings, the author).

By now the rain had ceased. As we neared the heart of the city, I suggested that we go to the Imperial Hotel, this being the only place besides the Emperor's palace I had heard of in Tokyo. Accordingly, we asked directions several times, and finally drove into a circular driveway in front of the Imperial. We climbed down from the truck and somewhat cautiously entered the doorway. We found it to be beautiful and modern in every respect (although part of one wing had been leveled by our bombs).

Approaching the desk, while being closely watched by every Japanese in the room, we politely inquired if we could get lunch. We were referred to the manager, a stockily-built Japanese, who hesitantly said that lunch would be served at 11:30. But he firmly denied our request for beer, stating it was unobtainable. We spent the next half hour remaining until lunch time looking over the hotel and getting our dollars and Philippine pesos changed into yens. We found the rate of exchange to be 15 yen to the dollar. (What a difference from today's rate.) Several correspondents made reservations for staying at the hotel later.

Promptly at 11:30, we filed into the dining room, careful not to check our pistols and carbines. We must have presented a strange sight to the few apparently higher class Japanese who were already seated. Several of these were army officers, but I was unable to determine their rank. The meal was well prepared but austere. It consisted of a reasonably good soup, broiled fish, some sort of stew with rice and heaven knows what kind of meat in it, and a pastry mixture of rice and flour which was served in the form of round balls. We were denied even one cup of tea, the only drink we had heard was available, except water.

As we were finishing eating, one of my public relations colleagues we had left in Yokohama entered the dining room, and came over to inform us that Tokyo had been placed "off limits" to all service personnel. He said that an order to this effect had been issued by General MacArthur a short time earlier, and that strict disciplinary action would be taken against any violators. So, being the senior officer, I rounded up our correspondents and prepared to leave immediately.

Despite the order, I couldn't resist riding a couple of blocks out of the way to get a glimpse of the Imperial Palace of his Imperial Majesty, the Emperor. We could not see much because of a moat and high wall which surrounds the palace grounds, but by craning our necks we did obtain a fair view of the palace. We did not see the Emperor's famed white horse, much to our disappointment.

Only one other incident took place that might be of interest. Just as we were leaving the suburbs on our return trip, we turned a blind corner into a main street and came upon a formation of Japanese soldiers, fully armed. Our correspondent-driver (I threatened to fire him later) went through some strange contortions with the steering wheel as though he was going to turn in another direction. But finally, at my urging, decided to face them. So, we rode down the long line of Japanese troops, less than five feet away, as if we were passing in review for them. Just as we reached the end of the line we nearly ran down their commander, apparently of high rank, who was sitting stiffly astride a beautiful roan horse while directing his troops. The horse was skittish, but no more than any of us at that stage, I'll wager.

JAPANESE IMPRESSIONS 18

M y first impressions of the Japanese — their appearance and their attitudes — were recorded in a personal column I wrote for a weekly newspaper soon after the war ended:

The Japanese are probably the best disciplined people on earth as evidenced by the fact that not one lifted a finger against us because of the emperor's order not to do so, whereas only a couple of weeks earlier it would have meant certain death for any American entering Japan for any reason.

Japan and the Japanese, as I saw them, reminded me more of Gilbert and Sullivan's "Mikado" than Puccini's "Madame Butterfly." As characters, the people in modern Japan were more of the comic opera type than the idealistic, highly sensitive persons depicted in the grand opera. Most of them were shabbily dressed and unkempt in appearance.

The women, in particular, seemed to care not in the least about their looks. But it would have done them little good to care. As a wartime measure, the Japanese government had decreed that all women wear slacks at all times in public. Consequently, you saw them only in slacks.

But these were not slacks as we know them. They were merely baggy trousers which had a balloon effect from the waist to the knees and then drew into a close fit at the ankles. A loose fitting blouse, usually of gaudy colors, completed the ensemble. The women had little femininity or charm, and paid not the slightest heed to us Americans.

This resulted — partially, at least — from a government order that women refrain from any contact with American occupation forces. The directive, issued just after we landed, warned the women that they must not smile or show the slightest sign of interest — or they would face the penalty of being criminally assaulted by us. The directive went further in explicitly pointing out that they must not smile or display any uncovered portions of their bodies.

"American and European women think nothing of exposing their backs and their feet," the order stated, "but we Japanese are more civilized than that. Do not expose any part of your body as that would incite the Americans to violence."

This was just one example of the many absurdities we saw on every hand.

The men seem to care just as little about their dress. They were, for the most part, poorly attired in ill-fitting costumes of every description. All of their clothes of the Western type were badly worn and usually dirty. I saw only two or three men dressed in what we would call passable suits and these were worn by men apparently of the highest class of society and the business world. It was not uncommon to see a man on the street with only a scanty loin cloth covering his body.

The column continued as follows by briefly describing other experiences and impressions which are written about in greater detail elsewhere in these pages:

As I went into Japan so early, I was able to see and participate in several of the history-making events that took place. But first I made an excursion into Tokyo that I wouldn't have gone on if I had thought the matter over carefully. This was on August 31 — the day after we arrived and two days before the surrender ceremony. There were no American forces there at the time and, looking back, it was a foolhardy adventure on my part. I was accompanied by another officer and 16 war correspondents and we rode in an open-body Japanese trucks. One hand grenade thrown by one fanatical Japanese would have been the same as if an atomic bomb had struck us.

I also witnessed the raising of the first American flag over Tokyo in nearly four years by a unit of the First Cavalry Division. But the event I was most fortunate to attend was the main one — the surrender ceremony aboard the battleship Missouri. And I had a ringside seat for this ceremony which brought an end to world strife — at least, temporarily. For me, this was a most dramatic and soul-stirring event. Yet, at the time, I seemed unable to grasp the historical significance of the words being said and the events taking place before me. It was an inspiring spectacle... one that I will cherish always...

Today, after more than 56 years, I find no reason to change my sentiments — even as emotionally charged as those words were.

A treasured memento presented to me in person by the general.

19
GENERAL MACARTHUR AS I KNEW HIM

"What do you really think of MacArthur?"

Through the years that question was asked of me more than any other by people who knew I was on his staff.

Usually, I could tell by the tone of voice how the questioner looked on the general, whether favorably or unfavorably. I have always listened courteously, and then tried to set them straight from my viewpoint, if we differed.

I am not going to rehash here some of the attacks leveled against him, and attempt to refute them, except to say that most of them were unfair and untrue, inspired by interservice jealousies. These have been aired to a considerable extent in the media and by word of mouth.

Suffice it to say, he treated me well. Although not a hero worshipper by nature, I admired and respected him.

While in Brisbane, a story told about Colonel Lloyd Lehrbas, aide to the general and one of my immediate superiors, helps to humanize MacArthur. Lehrbas, a former Associated Press writer who won high praise for his reporting during the fall of Poland, had worked for MacArthur in Washington when the general was army chief of staff. MacArthur had sent for him to come to Australia and serve on his press staff, as he had in Washington. He was given the rank of lieutenant colonel, wearing the distinctive aide shield with four stars, and later was promoted to full colonel.

Another colonel on MacArthur's staff related that Larry, as we called him, somehow had injured his right foot and was limping. The colonel jokingly remarked, in MacArthur's presence, that Larry had injured his foot by kicking a blonde out of bed. "Not likely," quickly retorted the general, "because Larry is left-footed." And Larry actually was left-footed, which MacArthur remembered from knowing him in Washington.

It was Larry who arranged my first head-to-head meeting with MacArthur, at Port Moresby, New Guinea, in 1944. In New Guinea, time "hung heavy," as the saying goes. One night I was sitting around reading — or perhaps wishing the war would end. It was probably the latter, since that was how I spend most of my spare time.

This night Larry came by my tent and asked if I would like to go with him to see General MacArthur, saying that he needed to confer with him. I gulped and said "yes" quickly, before he could withdraw the invitation.

We walked about a hundred yards through the lush tropical growth and came to a white house which, of course, GIs had dubbed "The White House," since it was both the general's head-quarters and living quarters. The house, a large, rambling bungalow, had been the residence of the colonial administrator. I will not attempt to describe the place further, except to say it was not imposing in appearance and the furnishings were spare and simple, in keeping with the hot climate.

As we entered, MacArthur was seated at a desk, with papers before him. He was alone, and fully clothed. Larry introduced us (I was a captain at the time), and we shook hands. He was cordial and friendly, inquiring as to my health and well being. And (can you imagine?), thanked me for serving under him. His conversation with Larry revolved around the wording of a communique due for release the next day. I don't remember the details but, as a censor and PR officer, I was interested in hearing how the question was resolved at such a high level.

By coincidence, a month or two later, Larry and MacArthur's communiques received nationwide newspaper play with an item appearing May 21, 1944 in the popular nationally syndicated column "Washington Merry-Go-Round" by Drew Pearson. Here's an excerpt from that column:

> When Colonel Larry Lehrbas, press aide to General MacArthur, returned to Washington recently he dropped in to greet old cronies at the State Department press room. Lehrbas has had a meteoric career, first as a cameraman in China, later as a Associated Press reporter

covering the State and War Departments. There he met MacArthur, and became his press adviser.

The ex-reporter explained that MacArthur's communiques, considered by the War Department to be the most "unusual" of any military commander, were first written by Lehrbas or one of the press officers and then sent up to MacArthur.

"However, MacArthur usually rewrites them," Larry explained. "Once he got the boys together and read a statement which he intended issuing to the press."

"'What do you think?' he asked, 'are those words too flamboyant? You know there are some people back in Washington who think I'm too theatrical'."

A few years ago in a creative writing course, we students were given an assignment to write an entire piece in dialogue only — just dialogue. Here's what I wrote, which serves to describe my final meeting with MacArthur in a rather unusual way:

A Dialogue About MacArthur

"Good morning."

"Sleep well?"

"Yes. How was your class?"

"It went well."

"What's your next assignment?"

"To write dialogue. It must be just dialogue. No description or background of any kind. Nothing but 'he said' or 'she said.' Oh, yes, there must be some resolution resulting from the dialogue."

"What will you write about?"

"Haven't decided. What do you suggest?"

"Um... um. How about a conversation between you and another person connected to one of your experiences in the army?"

"A good idea. I might write about meeting and talking with General MacArthur just before leaving Japan for home in October 1945. This would tie in with my association with him, and give me a chance to describe him. This might be interesting to some people."

"Just what did MacArthur say, and what was his appearance and demeanor?"

"He said nothing profound. But he did look handsome and stern, just like the pictures you see. And you could tell he covered his large bald spot with a shock of hair."

"Of course, he was immaculate, dressed in a clean, sharply pressed, apparently tailored, khaki uniform. His collar was open, and the five-star circular insignia was worn on either side."

"Was he smoking his famous corncob pipe?"

"No, but I did see it on an ash tray on his desk, and occasionally he glanced at it longingly."

"He greeted us (three of us who had served on his staff for several years) cordially, and said he appreciated our loyalty and devotion to duty."

"Then he said in his deep, resonant voice, with dramatic overtones: 'One of the saddest things in the military is when friends are forced to part.'"

"Before leaving, he presented each of us with an autographed photograph, which we had requested earlier."

"Our teacher's rather cranky. Hope this qualifies as a resolution of what to write about."

Released to the Press at 12:00 Noon 11th December 1942.

Edmund C. Hughes
Capt., Inf.
(For) L. A. DILLER
Colonel, Press Relations

G.H.Q. SOUTHWEST PACIFIC AREA
COMMUNIQUE NO. 243 DEC. 11, 1942

NORTHWESTERN SECTOR

Activity limited to reconnaissance.

NORTHEASTERN SECTOR

NEW GUINEA:

The Gona area has been completely occupied by our forces. A night counter-attack by the enemy in the Buna area collapsed under our fire. Bitter hand-to-hand fighting ensued throughout the position in the struggle for pill-box type, enemy machine-gun emplacements. Our air force continued direct support action.

One of several official communiques I signed for Colonel Diller.

THE SURRENDER CEREMONY

In the pre-dawn darkness, we awoke with an awareness of impending excitement. We were at an unpretentious hotel in Yokohama where we in public relations of MacArthur's headquarters were staying since arriving in Japan three days earlier.

It was September 2, 1945, the historic date of the Japanese surrender ceremony.

We dressed quickly in the dim light, ate a hurried breakfast of K-rations (notwithstanding a lingering fish smell), and were driven in a dilapidated Japanese bus to a dock area on Tokyo Bay.

The morning dawned with a gray overcast as we boarded the destroyer Taylor to be transported to the battleship Missouri, six miles out in Tokyo Bay. Aboard were 194 correspondents, representing all the major news media of the world.

At 8:55 a.m., just after we had gone aboard the battleship and found our assigned places for viewing the ceremony, the U.S. destroyer Landsdowne, bearing the 11-man Japanese contingent, came alongside.

The Japanese were accompanied by Colonel Sidney F. Mashbir, a U.S. Army officer, who was serving as interpreter and guide. Colonel Mashbir, lank and handsome, well over six feet tall, appeared in striking contrast to the diminutive Japanese.

The assemblage was silent as the stony-faced Japanese climbed the steep gangway and slowly advanced towards the old iron chow table, covered with a baize-colored felt cloth, which held the surrender documents.

Four civilians, led by Foreign Minister Mamoru Shigemitsu, and seven uniformed Japanese, headed by General Yoshijiro Umezu, chief of the Imperial General Staff, comprised the delegation. Shigemitsu wore formal attire, even to a top hat and white gloves, which lent a slightly comic opera aspect to the spectacle.

RANDOM SHOTS ABOARD THE BATTLESHIP MISSOURI
AT SURRENDER CEREMONY

I'm in upper left gun turret.

Well dressed for the occasion.

Are these Chinese or Russians?

Strolling on deck, so to speak.

View approaching the Missouri.   Military men of every stripe.

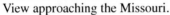

The sullen-looking General Umezu wore an ill-fitting green uniform. He had voiced strong opposition to capitulation.

Foreign Minister Shigemitsu, whose slight, shrunken figure was supported by a cane, hobbled at such a slow pace, and with such difficulty, across the deck that I instinctively wanted to assist him.

Surrounding the table by which the Japanese stood were many of the highest ranking military officers of all the allied nations engaged in the war. Closely packed as they were, their uniforms formed a patchwork quilt of variegated hues and patterns. Some were in full dress uniform, bedecked with ribbons and medals. Other uniforms, like MacArthur's and members of his staff, were unadorned except for insignia of rank and service.

A sea of eyes swept over the scene on the quarterdeck.

Spectators filled all available space in that area of the 45,000-ton ship. They were hanging from the railings, arms and legs draping over the bulwarks of the big 16-inch guns. They were leaning against the stanchions, lining the catwalks, jamming the gun turrets, and standing on the capstans.

Faces peered in from all directions.

After a few minutes' wait, General MacArthur stepped briskly forward to face the Japanese. He was followed by five-star Admiral Chester Nimitz and Admiral William F. Halsey. MacArthur read a brief statement explaining the purpose of the occasion, and then directed that the signing be accomplished.

First to sign were Shigemitsu and Umezu. MacArthur signed next as allied commander followed by Nimitz for the United States and, in order, representatives of China, the United Kingdom, the Soviet Union, Australia, Canada, France, the Netherlands and New Zealand.

Perched in a lofty, crowded gun turret, I viewed the entire proceedings, observing the slight tremor in MacArthur's hands as he read his stirring statement. He said, in part: "It is my solemn hope and indeed the hope of all mankind that from this solemn occasion a better world shall emerge out of the blood and carnage of the past — a world founded upon faith and understanding — a world dedicated to the dignity of man and the fulfillment of his most cherished wish — for freedom, tolerance and justice."

I was struck then, as I still am today, by the stern warning expressed in a radio broadcast he made to the world immediately following the ceremony:

"We have had our last chance. If we do not now devise some greater and more equitable system, Armageddon will be at our door.

... It must be of the spirit if we are to save the flesh."

Thus, World War II—the bloodiest conflict mankind has ever known—officially ended.

Reproduced on the next two pages is a copy, front and back, of the "Instrument of Surrender." Shown here in reduced size because of space limitations, the historic document was also written in Japanese and signed by the same representatives.

INSTRUMENT OF SURRENDER

W e, acting by command of and in behalf of the Emperor of Japan, the Japanese Government and the Japanese Imperial General Headquarters, hereby accept the provisions set forth in the declaration issued by the heads of the Governments of the United States, China and Great Britain on 26 July 1945, of Potsdam, and subsequently adhered to by the Union of Soviet Socialist Republics, which four powers are hereafter referred to as the Allied Powers.

We hereby proclaim the unconditional surrender to the Allied Powers of the Japanese Imperial General Headquarters and of all Japanese armed forces and all armed forces under Japanese control wherever situated.

We hereby command all Japanese forces wherever situated and the Japanese people to cease hostilities forthwith, to preserve and save from damage all ships, aircraft, and military and civil property and to comply with all requirements which may be imposed by the Supreme Commander for the Allied Powers or by agencies of the Japanese Government at his direction.

We hereby command the Japanese Imperial General Headquarters to issue at once orders to the Commanders of all Japanese forces and all forces under Japanese control wherever situated to surrender unconditionally themselves and all forces under their control.

We hereby command all civil, military and naval officials to obey and enforce all proclamations, orders and directives deemed by the Supreme Commander for the Allied Powers to be proper to effectuate this surrender and issued by him or under his authority and we direct all such officials to remain at their posts and to continue to perform their non-combatant duties unless specifically relieved by him or under his authority.

We hereby undertake for the Emperor, the Japanese Government and their successors to carry out the provisions of the Potsdam Declaration in good faith, and to issue whatever orders and take whatever action may be required by the Supreme Commander for the Allied Powers or by any other designated representative of the Allied Powers for the purpose of giving effect to that Declaration.

We hereby command the Japanese Imperial Government and the Japanese Imperial General Headquarters at once to liberate all allied prisoners of war and civilian internees now under Japanese control and to provide for their protection, care, maintenance and immediate transportation to places as directed.

The authority of the Emperor and the Japanese Government to rule the state shall be subject to the Supreme Commander for the Allied Powers who will take such steps as he deems proper to effectuate these terms of surrender.

Signed of _____ TOKYO BAY, JAPAN _____ at _____ 0904 T _____

on the _____ SECOND _____ day of _____ SEPTEMBER _____ , 1945

重 光 葵

By Command and in behalf of the Emperor of Japan
and the Japanese Government.

梅 津 美 治 郎

By Command and in behalf of the Japanese
Imperial General Headquarters.

Accepted at _____ TOKYO BAY, JAPAN _____ at _____ 0908 T _____

on the _____ SECOND _____ day of _____ SEPTEMBER _____ , 1945

for the United States, Republic of China, United Kingdom and the Union of Soviet Socialist Republics, and in

the interests of the other United Nations at war with Japan.

Douglas MacArthur
Supreme Commander for the Allied Powers

C.W. Nimitz
United States Representative

徐永昌
Republic of China Representative

Bruce Fraser
United Kingdom Representative

Kuzma Derevyanko
Union of Soviet Socialist Republics
Representative

T.A. Blamey
Commonwealth of Australia Representative

Moore Cosgrave
Dominion of Canada Representative

Leclerc
Provisional Government of the French
Republic Representative

M. Helfrich
Kingdom of the Netherlands Representative

Leonard M. Isitt
Dominion of New Zealand Representative

Post-War Appendage

"Old soldiers never die or fade away — they attend reunions."

That line, paraphrasing MacArthur's classic closing of his 1951 speech to Congress, I am stealing from a feature article by a former colleague, Selwyn Pepper, in the *St. Louis Post-Dispatch*.

The subject of that article was the one and only reunion of members of MacArthur's wartime public relations staff, held in October 1985 at Bradenton, Florida. Some 20 people gathered for the two-day event, including wives and one ex-war correspondent — Bill Dunn, formerly of CBS, who had been a personal friend of MacArthur's

The whole affair was a tribute to Brigadier General LeGrande A. (Pick) Diller, our big boss and MacArthur's PR chief throughout the war years and afterwards. He served as an aide-de-camp to him, and was highly regarded and respected by correspondents and members of his own staff alike.

Another reunion scheduled two years later at the MacArthur Memorial in Norfolk, Virginia, was canceled due to the death of General Diller on September 2, 1987 at age 86. In a letter to me, dated November 19, 1985, the general said he looked forward to the next reunion, and added: "We love Norfolk... the Memorial means a lot to me. I always feel as if the Old Man is just around the corner when I'm there."

An elaborate program had been planned for the second reunion, with Mrs. MacArthur in attendance as a special honored guest. I was eagerly anticipating seeing her again and, this time, meeting her. My one encounter with Mrs. MacArthur occurred when I was on the same elevator with her at Lennon's Hotel in Brisbane, Australia, where I stayed for a short time. (The MacArthurs had a suite there, which happened to be near my room. Often, during the early morning hours, I heard their young son, Arthur, playfully yelling. This was particularly unwelcome after a stint of nighttime censoring duty, or other nocturnal activity.) That day on the elevator, Mrs. MacArthur smiled and spoke to me. Obviously, she was a charming and gracious lady.

In June 1993, I received a letter from Colonel Lyman H. Hammond, Jr., executive director of the General Douglas MacArthur Foundation at Norfolk. He stated, in part: "For some time now, I have been collecting documents and photographs from those correspondents attached to SWPA (Southwest Pacific Area) and from those people on Diller's staff. The purpose of this letter is to ask you to donate anything you might have on this important period in history to us or, if not us, some other institution who will preserve the items."

I replied that I had no material that I felt would be appropriate to donate, and went on to inform him I was writing my autobiography and that if, in the process, I discovered anything suitable, I would forward it to him. Thus far, no success.

Incidentally, Colonel Hammond mentioned in his letter that a close friend and former West Point classmate of his, Jim Tormey, was the son of Colonel Bernie Tormey, who was on MacArthur's staff. "You probably knew him," he wrote.

Colonel Tormey, who as chief censor was my immediate superior, figures briefly in an article titled "The Haugland Story," appearing elsewhere in these pages. This deals with my involvement in a censorship mix-up which went all the way up to MacArthur for adjudication, with Diller and Tormey personally escorting me to his office. The general's decision saved my job as a censor.

GENERAL HEADQUARTERS
UNITED STATES ARMY FORCES, PACIFIC
PUBLIC RELATIONS OFFICE

ADVANCE ECHELON,
APO 500,
26 September 1945.

Dear Ed,

    I want you to know in writing how much I appreciate
the loyal support you always gave. I could always feel
that I not only could depend upon you, but when you were
on duty, the job would be well and carefully done. We had
some great times together through a long, trying period.
Without the help of my team, we never could have made it
a success.

    This letter brings to you my sincere best wishes for
continued success.

    With kindest regards.

Yours sincerely,

L. A. DILLER,
Brigadier General, GSC.

Major Edmund C. Hughes,
Marietta, Georgia.

A much-appreciated post-war letter from General Diller.

HAROLD MARTIN

Looks Forward

To Coming Home

TOKYO.

Dear Josh:

I was around the other night when Tojo shot himself, and your newspaperman's soul would have delighted to see the boys start working an old-fashioned story of the police type again. Most of them had been writing from handouts and from conducted tours and formal interviews for a long time but when the story broke they went after it like cubs going to a fire.

Some of them were standing a watch outside his house when he shot himself and they went tearing in with the photographers and the old rascal lay there with the blood bubbling out, with the guys taking notes and the flash bulbs going like heat lightning. I don't suppose an attempted suicide has ever been covered any better. One GI driver, though, didn't care much for the news end of it. A practical man, a souvenir grabbing veteran, no doubt, of many campaigns, he merely filched the old so-and-so's ceremonial sword and beat it back to the jeep, where he sat, looking innocent, until the boys came out to be rushed back to the hotel. And, as always happens, when a big one breaks fast, two of the gang, trying, naturally, to be in first, thought a faint was the real thing and rushed back to flash that Tojo was dead. It was probably the only time in history that a censor has been cussed for working too fast.

MAJOR ED HUGHES, who used to be with Otis Brumby up at Marietta, handled the copy, and when they rushed back, blowing their tops, to kill the flash, he had already passed the story on to be transmitted and it was probably in LA by that time. And speaking of Mariettans, I saw Mongin Brumby around the hotel. He's with one of the radio chains now and had just come in from Hongkong, where he went with the British, I believe he said.

ITS BEEN a pretty dull occupation so far. The geisha houses get a big play in the evening, with everybody going down to sip tea and watch the dancers and listen to somebody strum on a three-stringed instrument called a samesin, which sounds like a banjo without enough strings on it. It's quite a novel experience but you get tired of it after the first time. You sit around on the floor with your shoes off and your legs doubled under you, which cripples a long-legged man after an hour. The houses are beautiful, paneled in all sorts of polished woods, with flower and bird paintings in the delicate Japanese manner all about, and the girls are pretty, too. I suppose, though, most of them somehow look like mice. The kimonos and obis are beautiful prewar stuff, wonderfully woven in colored designs and I wish I could buy a new one to bring home. But every GI who visits a geisha house has the same idea, I understand, and the answer so far has been a polite but firm "No Soap." Somebody is going to show up with a couple of pounds of sugar though and walk off with everything in the house, for the Japs are very short of sugar and they love it dearly.

MY MAIN impression of a geisha establishment was the first one. I ducked my head to enter the room where the dancers perform and there were tiny people sitting around the little tables, sipping tea from tiny cups, and a dancer about the size of my thumb twirling in the corner, and I had the strange feeling that I had stepped into a very beautifully furnished doll's house, where a scene from a book of fairy stories was being enacted.

BUT THE HOUR grows late and I must crawl now into one of those tiny little beds which cause tall Americans so much trouble in these parts. This hotel was built, they say, for the Olympic games of 1940, which were to be held in Tokyo but never came off. I don't know who was to occupy this room. Probably a swimming team made up of Singer midgets. The bed is at least a foot shorter than I, and the bath tub I can hardly get both feet in at once, and to see in the mirror to shave I have to get down on my knees. Even the trains look like scale models. I rode from Tokyo to Yokohama the other day, standing up, naturally, and though the train was a fast, smooth riding electric it swayed a little on the turns and to steady myself I would reach up and place my hand flat against the ceiling. This caused a great jabbering among the people. I felt like Gulliver in Lilliput.

I HAVE TO MAKE a short trip into China to see some Marines over there. After that I hope it's home with a stop at Pearl Harbor only long enough to grab some decent clothes which I left there for the moths to munch on while I was gone.

Regards,   MARTIN.

(Written July 18, 1994)

Postscript

I was saddened to read in an Atlanta newspaper last week the obituary of Harold Martin, 82, long-time *Atlanta Constitution* columnist and a former *Saturday Evening Post* editor.

Harold, a fellow-alumnus of UGA's journalism school, and then a World War II Marine combat correspondent, looked me up in Tokyo and said he wanted to visit a geisha house, asking if I would arrange for a staff car and accompany him.

The letter above and on preceding page, clipped from the *Atlanta Constitution*, describes that visit.

Explanation: I approved the story about Tojo's "death" because I had no reason to question its validity.

Two images of Harold Martin stand out in my memory: his gyrations while attempting to bathe in the small tub in my room at the Dai-ichi Hotel; and, his appearance while dancing shoeless with a costumed geisha girl one third his size.

Ah, such memories!

RETURN TO MARIETTA AND CIVILIAN LIFE

Throughout my extended overseas army duty, I never gave serious consideration to following any post-war course other than returning to Marietta and resuming employment with the Brumby publishing firm. In correspondence with Otis Brumby, I was assured a suitable position would be available for me after the war. Consequently, I did not explore some potential opportunities that came my way. These included a request from an Atlanta printing company executive, whom I met while on home leave, that I make no employment commitment before consulting him.

It happened that just before I left army service, Otis had suffered a severe heart attack and was unable to continue in active management of the business, forcing his wife, Elisabeth, to take control on a part-time basis while also caring for him.

When I arrived home in late October and was placed on terminal leave at Fort McPherson, I was immediately called to Marietta for an interview with Robert Brumby, lawyer brother of Otis, who had been summoned from his home in Louisiana to negotiate my hiring and to handle other legal matters pertaining to the company. I felt comfortable meeting with him, since I had known him before when he had lived in Marietta, and incidentally, had dated his daughter, Roberta, a few times.

"Mr. Bob," as I called him, and I quickly came to an agreement: I was to be in complete charge of the business with the title of general manager at a salary of $100 per week. Also, I would receive stock representing 10% ownership of the business. A written contract to this effect was drawn up and signed.

At the same time, Leo Aikman, who was well established as editor of the *Cobb County Times*, was given a contract with the same terms relating to ownership.

It should be explained here that the main business of Brumby Press was the printing of trade magazines, which accounted for about 80% of the company's volume. These included: *Southern Automotive Journal, Electrical South*, and *Laundryman's Guide*. This meant that between 50 and 60 employees were needed to produce them and the newspaper, plus a small amount of routine job printing.

I was the general manager of both the *Times* and Brumby Press, but with so capable an editor as Leo, I was able to devote virtually full time to management duties. This was especially helpful at the beginning when I started learning the nuts and bolts of publication printing, as well as refreshing what I already knew about it.

Leo, while a National Park Service historian at nearby Kennesaw National Park, had joined the *Times* staff as editor during the war years. He was an immediate success, I was happy to learn, and carried on the paper's tradition of excellence. A native of Indiana, he was an honor graduate of DePauw University in that state. Another distinction: He was born and grew up in the small town of Dana, the homeplace of Pulitizer Prize-winning war correspondent Ernie Pyle. Leo's mother and Pyle's mother were friends.

Leo's personal column, "And Selected Short Subjects," was widely read because of its home-spun humor. With humor as his hallmark, Leo began accepting speaking engagements and eventually developed into one of the most popular speakers in and around Atlanta. In fact, he received many honorariums and did quite well financially.

A typical example of Leo's humorous oratory delivered with a deadpan expression:

An Army recruit was suspected of being mentally deficient, and was being questioned by a psychiatrist to determine his fitness for service.

"What would happen if I cut off one of your ears?" the psychiatrist asked.

"I probably couldn't hear as well," the recruit replied.

"What would happen if I cut off both your ears?" the

doctor inquired.

"I couldn't see," he answered.

"What do you mean, you couldn't see?" demanded the questioner.

"Because my hat would fall down over my eyes," came the reply.

Another sample of Leo's speech-making humor:

A Yankee tourist stopped at a Cobb County service station and began a conversation with the attendant.

"Cobb County, eh? Any big men born here?"

"Nope," the attendant replied, "only babies. Guess they do it different up North."

Leo's speeches and writing had more than humor as their base. They were interlarded with down-home philosophy and advice for living well.

Leo was also called on to introduce other speakers at various meetings and functions. On one occasion he was asked to introduce the prominent publisher of the *Atlanta Constitution*, Ralph McGill. Leo put a fresh and different twist on the introduction, as only Leo could do.

Leo pre-planned the stratagem with the connivance of Ralph McGill.

When the time came for the introduction, Leo stood up and proclaimed, "You have often heard it said a speaker needs no introduction; such is the case tonight." With that he abruptly sat down and McGill rose immediately and began his speech.

The stunt worked because everyone in the audience was acquainted with Ralph McGill from reading his daily column in the *Constitution*.

Two years later, Leo would resign as editor of the *Times* to accept an offer from Ralph McGill to join the *Constitution* editorial staff as a daily columnist. This he did successfully for several years until his death in the 1960s.

During this period, I also made speeches (without remuneration, of course) to various civic groups recounting my war experiences. These included the Marietta Kiwanis Club, the

Marietta Woman's Club, and the Cartersville Rotary Club. But the highlight of my brief speaking schedule was an address to the student body of the University of Georgia School of Journalism at the invitation of Dean John E. Drewry.

I made another speech on Confederate Memorial Day, April 26, 1946, sponsored by the Ladies Memorial Association and the Kennesaw Chapter of the United Daughters of the Confederacy, to a sizeable audience at the Cobb County courthouse on the square in Marietta.

The occasion served as a tribute to the Civil War dead of the Confederacy. Many prominent citizens, including all the local political leaders, were always on hand. This was especially true in Cobb County, which had been a battleground for much fierce fighting. In researching my speech, I boned up on Civil War history and learned more about that tragic struggle. How different from World War II. Today, Confederate Memorial Day is observed by only a handful of the ever-faithful. I remember typing that speech and reading it to the audience. Here are some excerpts:

> Today, it is as befitting as at any time in history since that earlier struggle took place that we join together to pay due homage and respect to the memories of our forefathers — those gallant men in gray who chose to fight and die for an ideal — a conviction.
>
> How well those same words exemplified the spirit of those who took part in the world conflict just ended. Instead of brother against brother, however, it was brother at the side of brother as Southerners and Northerners — Americans all — faced the common foe. And how well they stood and fought together — and, yes, died together.
>
> The scars of that earlier struggle have healed now, but time has not dimmed the bravery of the men whose memory we honor here today.
>
> I would point out to you that that same spirit of fierce independence, those same qualities of individual initiative, resourcefulness, and self-reliance which characterized our forefathers — these same qualities are the ones

which enabled us to crush our ruthless foreign enemies on two successive occasions.

That spirit, which is our heritage, has meant the difference between being conquered and overrun by aggressor nations, or being victorious, and thus maintaining our principles of righteousness and justice.

(In closing) The real hope humanity now possesses rests in the United Nations organization and in the willingness and capacity of governments to put it to work. Our leading statesmen, including President Truman, believe that if the United Nations is now utilized to the fullest extent by all participating countries, it can lay the foundations for world reconstruction, for human progress, and for peace among nations.

As we go forth from this Confederate Memorial Day of 1946, let us prayerfully hope that these aims will be accomplished so that mankind henceforth may live in peace and happiness.

Since Otis' illness, his personal column, "Jambalaya," had been written by several people pinch-hitting for him, including Leo at times. As I've stated before, Otis' column had been the most outstanding feature of the newspaper since the paper's inception, and I felt highly complimented when Otis asked that I take over the writing of Jambalaya on a regular basis. I quickly accepted the challenge and began what would continue on a weekly basis for five years. On the next pages my first effort is reproduced, in full.

I soon realized my job demanded a much wider range of responsibility than had my pre-war position with the firm. As the "boss," I was charged with keeping everyone satisfied, including the employees as well as our customers — the publishers of the trade magazines we printed.

Shortly after my take-over, an incident involving the employees helped to solidify my position and made me feel I had their confidence. This resulted from an attempt by two Atlanta labor unions to organize our employees into union members.

As 'HUGHES VIEWS'

JAMBALAYA

(Originated by Otis A. Brumby in January, 1934)

By Edmund C. Hughes

Five Years Is A Long Time

"OCCUPIED." They can take down the "For Rent" sign over this column now. This space in your favorite newspaper has been without a regular tenant ever since Publisher Otis A. Brumby became ill last April. Meanwhile, Editor Leo Aikman has turned in a sterling job of pinchhitting for the "boss". But one column per person per week is enough, says Editor Leo, and I am of the same opinion, especially when I am manning the typewriter.

This is the column I've been waiting for five years to write. Not necessarily in this particular spot of the newspaper do I mean, but I have been waiting that long to dabble these hands in printer's ink again. And, of course, I mean in the TIMES own special brand of printer's ink which I found nowhere else in my army travels. Five years is a long time by any standard of measurement, even when you are at home among friends and familiar scenes, but away from home it becomes almost like eternity. Or so it seems. To say that I am glad to be back will be trite, but I am going to be trite and say it anyway, and add that I hope it's "for keeps" now.

Hallmark of Quality

Publisher Brumby started writing this column 12 years ago, and since that time it has been without a doubt the most widely-read of any feature of the entire newspaper. And deservedly so. But you readers know that better than I.

Jambalaya, even though the origin and meaning of the word itself has remained a mystery to some of its readers throughout the years, is one of the hallmarks which has given this paper the widespread recognition it has received throughout the nation. Just as the masthead at the top of this page announces the name of the newspaper in its distinctive outline letters, so has the title Jambalaya, week after week, symbolized the character and integrity of the newspaper.

But obviously, from the contents of Jambalaya has sprung its popularity. Publisher Brumby has always had that rare gift of writing just as though he were actually talking or chatting with you, but still always in clear, forceful language. You have always known how he stood on a particular issue or question. He has always been forthright and to the. point. You have seen him "point with pride" and "view with alarm", just as any editorial columnist does, but Jambalaya has consistently maintained a distinctive flavor of its own.

That brings us to the question of what Jambalaya actually does mean and how it originated. But first, let me say that in taking over Jambalaya I am attempting to fill some mighty big shoes and that I will try to maintain in some measure the high standard Publisher Brumby has set.

Here is how and when the column was started, as I discovered from looking at our files of back issues: The first column Otis wrote was under the date of January 25, 1934, without a name. He simply placed six big question marks over it and announced in the column that it was too early to name such an infant and stating that maybe some reader could offer a suggestion for a name.

In the next issue he revealed in the opening sentence, "The baby has been named," and carried the heading Jambalaya for the first time. But he refused to tell what the word itself meant, stating that the first person to define the word correctly would receive a gift. In two issues following this he announced the winner—Mrs. C. C. Folsom, Smyrna, RFD, who wrote from a sick bed. Rather than quote her definition, however, I am going to reproduce what Otis said at the time and give you his brother Bob's definition:

"Several friends wish to know why I selected this name to head my column. It was this way. When I attended college—Tulane at New Orleans—our yearbook was called JAMBALAYA. It had everything about college life in it. Just as the Blue Print at Tech and Pandora at Georgia cover everything in connection with college life in these institutions. As I do not intend to write on any one subject, I could not think of a suitable name other than one in common use in newspapers all around us. I do not claim in using the word Jambalaya to head my column that I have used it in an original sense, for it would not be surprising if it has not been used in Louisiana at some time or other, but at the present time there is no one writing under this head as far as I know. To be sure that the name would be suitable to head my column I wrote my brother Bob out in Louisiana about the word and how I intended using it. Here is Bob's interpretation:

'The word, 'Jambalaya' as I understand it, means a mixture of a good many things thrown in a pot with some rice. In other words, the basis of the dish is rice, and after that you put in ham, or turkey, or oysters, or anything else that you want to in the way of a solid food. It is, therefore, a variable dish in flavor based on the rice as a foundation. In this sense, I think the name would be appropriate for your column.' "

Thanks, Friends

Now I wish to thank my old friends and friends of Bosses Otis and Elisabeth for the encouraging words and kind treatment I have received on every hand since my return. It all has been really gratifying, and I thank you most heartily. A number of friends have called and been by to see me, but there are others I still have not had the opportunity of seeing.

Getting back into harness this first week has required virtually all of my time, but now that I am gradually getting more into the swing of things I will be able to get out and around more.

Among the veterans around Marietta, many of whom have been away about as long as I have, I was pleased to see Jimmy Hancock, Claud Hicks, Ebbie Lance, Jr., Luther Hames, Grover Fennell, Jim Dawson, and several others. And just this morning Rosser Little came by for a welcome chat. I was happy to notice that all of them were looking fine and fit and none the worse for their having been in the service. In most instances, these boys appeared to be in even better health than when I knew them before. But the best part of it is that they have been able to take up their lives where they left off—and make a go of it.

In next week's column I will write of my experience during the initial stages of the occupation of Japan and present my views on how General MacArthur has carried out the occupation and the background behind some of his more recent moves in clamping down on the Japanese.

Otis Brumby had always maintained an open shop, paying wages at least equal to the union wage scale in Atlanta, and I was determined to continue that policy.

One afternoon two men came to the back door of the plant and started talking to employees. I confronted them and invited them to my office. They introduced themselves as officers of the Atlanta Typographical Union and the Atlanta Pressman's Union, and stated: "We're going to organize your employees."

"Maybe so," I said, "but you're going to do it outside the plant."

That night, I learned on good authority that an organizational meeting had been held as scheduled, but not a single one of our employees had attended.

(Ironically, several years later, a crippling labor strike closed the doors of Brumby Press forever. This was two years after I left to join an Atlanta printing firm.)

During my stint as general manager, a succession of persons were hired to assist Leo in producing the newspaper. These included Frank Wesley, a UGA journalism graduate, who served

EDITORS HONORED—Newspaper people from throughout the State were honored for outstanding achievement in various fields of journalism at the annual convention of the Georgia Press Association. Shown above with their trophies are, first row, A. W. Starling, Nashville Herald, Sam W. Wilks Trophy; Albert Hardy, Jr., Commerce News, W. G. Sutlive Trophy; Mrs. Nora L. Smith, Ashburn Wiregrass Farmer, National Conference Christians and Jews Award; Ryan Frier, Bartow Herald (tied first place), Emory Journalism Department Award; F. T. Methvin, Eastman Times-Journal, Theron S. Shope Trophy; Edmund C. Hughes, the Brumby Press, which publishes Cobb County Times. Back row, Milton Fleetwood, Cartersville Tribune-News (tied for first place), Emory Journalism Department Award; A. L. Lee, Dalton News, J. C. Williams Trophy; Jim Coleman, Bulloch Herald, H. H. Dean Trophy; Leo Aikman and Frank Wesley, both of the Cobb County Times, Hal M. Stanley Trophy and W. Trox Bankston Trophy. The editors held their meeting at Jekyll Island.

Carrying on the tradition established by Otis Brumby, the *Cobb County Times* continued to win awards for outstanding achievement sponsored by the Georgia Press Association. The above photo, appearing in the *Atlanta Constitution*, pictures Leo Aikman, Frank Wesley and myself with the other winners.

as news editor, and Lyman Hall, as advertising manager. But the most noteworthy, Paul Thompson, who had the title of managing editor, stirred controversy with his style of writing and choice of material.

One example: When Virginia Hill, girlfriend of Bugsy Siegel, the notorious California gangster who was brutally slain with much attendant national publicity, came to Marietta to visit her mother in rural Cobb County, Paul recognized her in Florence's Department Store and attempted to interview her. I squelched the idea when I realized the implications of such a story appearing in a weekly newspaper. After all, we weren't a tabloid.

Paul was aggressive and crusading in covering the news, but often disregarded objectivity in his reporting. He was adept at concealing this, and we were forced to handle some of his material with caution. Leo would refer any questionable matter to me and I would often have to tone down or kill it, utilizing my army censorship experience to the fullest.

Ed Hughes, General Manager; Leo Aikman, Editor; and Lyman Hall, Advertising Manager, study a lay-out for the Cobb County Times, the nation's best weekly newspaper.

Above is the reproduction of a photograph appearing on the June 1946 cover of the *Editor's Forum*, official publication of the Georgia Press Association, attesting to a second national General Excellence award won by the *Cobb County Times*. The first came in 1938 when I was managing editor.

Throughout this time Leo and I both actively engaged in civic and political affairs while carrying on our regular duties. One year Leo served as president of the Marietta Rotary Club. Then I was elected to head the Kiwanis Club. He also served a term on the board of managers of the Georgia Press Association. Later I was appointed to that same position.

I also served one year as county chairman of the March of Dimes and was asked to become a member of the board of directors of the Cobb County Red Cross, but left Marietta before I could serve.

BOARD OF MANAGERS
(By Congressional District

Terms
Expire
1st—M. F. Clark, Jr. Hinesville 1950
2nd—E. C. Smith, Jr.,
    Donalsonville   1950
3rd—Byron C. Anglin, Richland 1951
4th—Berrien McCutchen,
    Franklin   1950
5th—Wright Bryan, Atlanta 1951
6th—W. H. Champion, Dublin 1950
7th—Edmund C. Hughes,
    Marietta   1951
8th—J. E. Baynard, Hazlehurst 1951
9th—Charles T. Graves,
    Clarkesville   1950
10th—Sanders Camp, Monroe 1951
Past President— J. W. Norwood,
    Lowndes County News, Valdosta

Board of Managers

Hughes	Baynard	Bryan	Anglin
Champion	McCutchen	Camp	Clark
Graves	Norwood	Frier	Hardy	Rountree

Another picture, appearing on the cover of the August 1949 issue of *Editor's Forum*, shows me with fellow board members. I was particularly impressed with Wright Bryan, editor of the *Atlanta Journal*, who had distinguished himself as a war correspondent in Europe, and was a prisoner of war for awhile.

Transition Time: Hopping From Little Pond to Big Pond

Despite my many ties to Marietta, I was not destined to continue working there as I had planned.

At the beginning of my five-year tenure as general manager, the Brumbys had requested that I move to Marietta to live, and I was reminded of this fact at various times. Just prior to my returning home from overseas, Frances had bought a house on Long Island Drive in Atlanta, and we were comfortable living there and resigned to my commuting daily to Marietta. Naturally, she was reluctant to move because of her singing career, centered in Atlanta, and she knew few people in Marietta.

I was ambivalent about moving since I liked Marietta and had many friends there. On the other hand, I respected Frances' wishes and understood her desire to remain in Atlanta.

When the Brumbys became adamant about our moving, a rift developed between us. If the truth be told, by this time I had become somewhat lackadaisical towards my work and found the job less interesting and challenging.

Looking back, another factor influenced this attitude — a deep-rooted concern that Otis, Jr., then a young boy, would one day be given the reins of the business, and I might be dismissed in the prime of my life.

Otis came up from his home in Florida and we had an open, heart-to-heart discussion in an Atlanta hotel room. The upshot was that I would resign and go with a printing firm in Atlanta. Chess Abernathy, my former associate at the *Cobb County Times*, who had just resigned as Alumni Secretary of Emory University, would succeed me.

My new job came about as the result of a visit to Higgins-McArthur Company, recognized as a leading printing firm throughout the Southeast. There I met with Kenton B. Higgins, owner of the company — in equal partnership with Richard N. McArthur, internationally known typographer and type designer. Mr. McArthur founded the company with Kent's father, Charlie Higgins, who was deceased.

When I asked Kent if he would be interested in my joining him, he graciously replied: "I would be honored to have you."

I had first met Kent a few years previously through Al Carson, manager of Whitaker Paper Company, which supplied paper to both Higgins-McArthur and Brumby Press. From this meeting evolved a regular monthly golf game with the three of us and one of Al's sales representatives playing different courses around the area.

So a twist of fate determined that I begin a fresh career in my former hometown of Atlanta. Thus, I changed from a big frog in a little pond to a little frog in a big pond. And the change became immediately refreshing and invigorating.

My new job was as a sales representative, but I worked under the same compensation plan as Kent and Mr. McArthur, with our income based completely on the amount of revenue we generated for the company. Strict cost accounting records were kept on each printing job and the results closely evaluated.

So we directed our efforts towards selling highly profitable printing. This usually required ingenuity and a certain creativeness. In fact, we called it "creative selling."

In getting started, I called on a number of old friends and acquaintances in a position to place printing of this type. These included former college mates and others I had known previously at various times.

As an interesting sidelight, my first important sale resulted from a tip supplied by Otis Brumby. He asked a mutual friend to call and inform me that printing of the *Southern Star*, employee publication of the Lockheed Corporation in Marietta, would be up for bid immediately. Otis had to give up printing the publication because of a labor strike that closed Brumby Press, and facilities at the *Marietta Daily Journal*, which he now published, were not suited for the job.

After successful competitive bidding, that publication, along with a multitude of other Lockheed work, became the mainstay of my career for more than 25 years.

Lee Rogers, director of public relations and a fellow-alumnus of the Georgia journalism school, who graduated a year earlier than I, directed and controlled the publishing of the *Southern Star*. Following graduation, he went to work for the *Atlanta Constitution* and rose to the position of managing editor before joining Lockheed.

I had known Lee casually at Georgia, and he seemed pleased that I had won the *Southern Star* contract. We became good friends and for many years worked on numerous successful Lockheed printing projects together, including an outstanding calendar which depicted a different Lockheed activity each month in original fine art paintings by Lockheed employee Maggie Wesley.

During this period I spent so much time at Lockheed that our young daughter, Lee Ann, once described me to a friend of hers like this: "He plays golf, but sometimes he goes to Lockheed." In my defense, I did play golf one afternoon a week and on the weekends when not working, but my work week still averaged more than 50 hours.

The *Southern Star* received many accolades for its overall excellence, especially during the editorship of Joe Dabney. One year during his stint, it was judged the best employee publication in the nation. Dabney became a best-selling author, writing two successful books before retiring — one about the making of corn whiskey and the other detailing the tremendous impact of the Lockheed designed-and-built C-130 Hercules. Just recently he won a prestigious award for his book on food preparation in the Appalachian mountains.

Before leaving Lockheed, I should reveal that Lee Rogers served as Assistant to the President under two different Lockheed presidents before his retirement.

We produced another award-winning Lockheed publication, *AirLifters*, a quarterly magazine, which besides providing service information, extolled the many virtues of the C-5 Galaxy, C-141 StarLifter, and C-130 Hercules as cargo-carrying aircraft.

Hy Abernathy headed the section that wrote and prepared the publication. I still have in my files a letter from Hy praising our efficiency and the quality of our printing. Bill Hammack, also a Georgia journalism school graduate, was one of the best writers I have known. That includes the war correspondents whose writing I read while serving as a military censor during World War II.

During this time Kent Higgins took me under his capable wing and inducted me into the world of quality printing. Mr. McArthur was much older, but contributed his part to my education, especially in the area of typography in advertising. He was widely recognized as the leading typographer in Atlanta and supplied much of the typesetting needs of the largest advertising agencies. This was long before the advent of the sophisticated computerized typesetting now in universal use.

Mr. McArthur used to proclaim constantly: "Concentrate on selling periodicals that are printed on a regular basis — weekly, semi-weekly, monthly, or quarterly. They work while you sleep." His advice proved invaluable.

I did as he said, and during my career I became known as a publication specialist. Publications I sold and serviced, in addition to the *Southern Star* and *AirLifters*, included *Southern Accents*, the *Economic Review*, *Parts Pups*, and *Colonial Ways*.

Southern Accents was the brain-child of Walter Mitchell, president of W.R.C. Smith Publishing Company. I sold him and Jim Lewis, his production manager, on our printing the quarterly magazine, beginning with the first issue in the Fall of 1978. As keepsakes, I still have copies, in mint condition, of two early issues. The publication became so successful that after two years it outgrew our equipment and was taken over by an out-of-town printer. Later, another publisher bought the magazine for what I understand was a large amount of money. Today, it rivals *Architectural Digest*, long recognized as the leader in the field.

A publication I more or less inherited after Mr. McArthur's death was the *Economic Review*, the prestigious "bible" of the financial community, published monthly by the Federal Reserve Bank of Atlanta. I handled this publication for more than 20 years, working closely with some fine, intelligent people while enjoying the financial benefits I received from my company.

Colonial Ways was a high-class employee publication put out by Colonial Stores, a large food chain of that era. This lasted for several years until Colonial discontinued the magazine after a merger with another chain.

The publication I enjoyed handling the most was *Parts Pups*, a monthly humor magazine published by Genuine Parts Company, a large automobile parts distributor. Through the years Don Kite, the editor, and I developed a rapport that transcended the business relationship and became a friendship that has lasted until the present time.

Being typographers naturally led to our designing and printing books of various types. I sold and handled several at different times. One was a religious treatise written in blank verse by LaBelle Lance, wife of Bert Lance, president Jimmy Carter's controversial budget director. The book, a small paperback, was titled "A Story from God." LaBelle was a nice lady, but not an accomplished writer, and needed all the help I could give her. We met regularly in the company conference room where she anguished over each change in her copy. I earned my commission on that job.

The first book I edited and produced was a slender, case-bound volume written by Dr. Jack Norris, a prominent Atlanta pathologist. The text in this book, titled "Gleanings From a Doctor's Eye," included numerous aphorisms, or short effective sayings, spread throughout its pages. Some were rather clever, some not so clever. I questioned the appropriateness of the title, but naturally he prevailed, as he should have.

In one chapter Dr. Norris recounted his experiences as a medical officer aboard a hospital ship anchored at Pearl Harbor during the treacherous Japanese attack on December 7, 1941. His description of that attack ranks as one of the best personal accounts of that tragedy I've read. (And I've just finished compiling and editing a book by Denver D. Gray featuring many such accounts, including a compelling one by the author himself.)

The Pearl Harbor episode was confined to only one chapter. Other chapters, with such headings as "Notes About Grandfather," "Man and His Health After 40," "Alcohol and Alcoholism," and "Will to Live and Will to Die," contained a varied assortment of down-to-earth homilies and homespun advice, interspersed with humor. The dedication reveals a wry sense of humor: "To My Wife, Elsa, Whose Criticism of This Book Cannot Be Printed."

The doctor distributed his book as gifts to friends and patients. In the introduction, he stated that, although being a doctor, he too feared becoming a cancer victim. Unfortunately and ironically, he died from that disease a few years after the book was published.

A more important book that I handled came my way through a referral by Brooks Smith, one of my successors at the Brumby-owned business in Marietta. Brooks published the *Marietta Daily Journal*, and Otis Brumby, Jr. later succeeded him in that position. The author of this book, retired Major General Haywood S. Hansell, of Hilton Head Island, S.C., commanded Air Force units that bombed Germany and Japan during World War II. He titled his opus "The Air Plan That Defeated Hitler."

MAJOR GENERAL HAYWOOD S. HANSELL, JR.
UNITED STATES AIR FORCE, RETIRED

For background: General Hansell commanded the Third Bombardment Wing and later the First Bombardment Division of the Eighth Air Force, which attacked German targets with B-17s. In 1944, he was named commander of the 21st Bomber Command of the 20th Air Force, which had B-29s at bases on Saipan and Guam. His unit dropped the first atomic bomb on Hiroshima in August 1945.

Despite his stature and high rank, General Hansell proved to be an affable gentleman who wrote quite well. Still, Harold Martin, long-time *Atlanta Constitution* columnist, was hired as editor and worked closely with us in polishing the copy. With my military experience and Harold's background as a Marine combat correspondent, we had a good working relationship with the general and he was pleased with the results. Here's the inscription in the signed copy he presented me:

The book was impressive, if I may be permitted to toss an accolade my way. Case-bound with a gold-stamped cover, it had a dust jacket printed in full color and featured original illustrations, including maps, designed by our company art department.

Incidentally, the book sold well and was used for awhile as a text book at the U.S. Air Force Academy. A second printing became necessary, and we readily obliged.

During these years, as busy as I was, I did not shirk my civic duty. This included activities both within and outside the printing industry.

In 1957-1958, I served on the board of the Printing Industry of Atlanta, a few years after Kent Higgins had been president. Mr. McArthur was also active in the organization, having founded an industry library named in his honor.

The Georgia Industrial Editors Association elected me president in 1963, and I thoroughly enjoyed holding this office for a group that included some of my best customers as members. An annual meeting in Athens highlighted each year.

Outside of the printing industry, I worked several years for the United Way and the American Red Cross. With the former, I solicited funds from various businesses and institutions. Eventually, I advanced to the point where I only recruited other fund raisers.

My involvement with the Red Cross consisted of serving on the public relations committee of the metro Atlanta chapter for four years. Kip Craven, director of public relations, was also active in the Industrial Editors Association.

It was during the early years of my employment at Higgins-McArthur that my marriage started to unravel. Strains began to develop that intensified and became acrimonious. Causes remain difficult to define. Trying to pinpoint the causes at this late date would be futile. However, I did not wish to dissolve the marriage, mainly because of the children.

Soon the breakup became inevitable, and after a couple of trial separations, I moved out. The divorce became final in 1953.

The children — Corrie, 11, and Jack, 8 — naturally were upset, but I visited them often and we consoled one another as best we could. I remember they particularly enjoyed what we called a "dark night" automobile ride, during which on a deserted road I would turn off the car's headlights and let it glide forward in the dark at a slow speed. It was harmless fun, and they never seemed to tire of it.

It should be reported here that Frances remarried within a year and moved to Macon with her physician-husband, who had been her doctor while she was student at nearby Wesleyan College.

For several years, I remained engrossed in my printing career. I had no real romantic interests, but I did date some.

Then one day in the Town House cafeteria on Forsyth Street in Atlanta, fate decreed that would change.

While eating lunch, as customary, with friends Bob Rankin and Gene McNeel, I saw an attractive-looking lady in the cafeteria line just ahead of us. I then remarked, spontaneously: "That's the kind of woman I would like to meet." Remembering this, Bob Rankin called me the next day saying he knew the lady, whose name was Eunice McGriff, and had invited her to have lunch with us that day.

The rest is history, as the pundits so blithely say. After my return from a brief Florida fishing trip, which I was committed to go on, we began dating, and soon were married.

While no marriage is perfect, ours has remained loving and eminently successful for just a few years short of a golden anniversary celebration. Our greatest joy still comes from our daughter, Lee Ann, now married with an outstanding husband and two charming children, Paul, 6, and Mary, 4. They live in Charlotte, N.C., but visit us often.

As for our social and recreational outlets, shortly after our marriage, I made one of the best moves of my life by joining Cherokee Town and Country Club. In 1956, we became charter members, paying a membership fee of only $650. I understand that fee recently went up to $50,000. What a bargain for us, even though we have "paid our dues" in the meantime.

For years, I played golf twice a week with great enjoyment, making many new friends while doing so. I also entertained customers at the club, both on and off the golf course. Although not really proficient at the game, I did score two holes-in-one, both on the same hole, seven years apart. Since giving up the game, we still enjoy dinner at the Town Club on a regular basis. Also, I exercise three times a week at the Town Club fitness center.

Now back to details of my business life.

Advertising agencies were prime sources for high-volume printing sales, and we catered to them in order to get our share of their business. One advantage of agency printing was it usually came copy-ready, or ready for production. On the other hand, this reduced the amount of the job's money volume. Another negative, some agencies secured three bids from reputable printers and went with the lowest bidder. (About this time a cartoon appeared in the media picturing a shabbily-dressed bum with the caption reading, "I was always the low bidder.")

I worked with the production managers, and sometimes the account executives, of several advertising agencies. These included: Burke Dowling Adams (they had the Delta Air Lines account), Lowe and Stevens (I was well acquainted with both partners), J. Howard Allison (whose Magic Chef stove account in Cleveland, Tenn., created a large volume of color printing), and Tucker & Associates (owner Susan Tucker became a close personal friend for several years and we enjoyed working on many projects together.)

When I first joined Higgins-McArthur, all of their pressroom equipment was letterpress for direct printing from type and engravings. This meant that to reproduce in 4-color process a form had to be run through the press four times, one for each color. In the late sixties, offset lithography, or indirect printing, was just coming into full vogue. At first we installed two 2-color presses, each capable of printing eight pages, size 8 1/2 x 11. These were more efficient, and made us more competitive in the market place, but they still lacked the advantages of some multi-color presses, geared up to produce five or six colors with one pass.

You can pull out all the stops in appraising my success. All the old cliches spring to mind: "Success breeds success," "The harder you work, the luckier you get." There never were truer sayings, and I believe I exemplified that fact. By then, the late fifties, I was making roughly $50,000 a year and that gradually increased as my clientele grew in number and my volume spiraled upward. In today's inflation-riddled economy what I earned would probably be worth at least triple what it was then.

My success, in addition to financial rewards, paid dividends in other tangible ways. In 1952, I was given the title "Vice President — Sales."

The title meant little except for the gain in prestige. I did hire two or three salesmen, but none panned out after frustrating periods of varying lengths. One of these who, as the art director and production manager of an advertising agency which went out of business, had been a customer of mine. He knew the technical aspects of printing well, but had little talent as a salesman.

In the early fifties we did hire a highly competent, experienced salesman who came by our office one afternoon and asked for a job. He was John MacKenzie, who decided to leave Foote & Davies, a rival firm, and join forces with us. John did well from the start and became a valuable addition to our firm. One he added to our account list was the Coca-Cola Company.

When Mr. McArthur died in 1956, his widow inherited his half of the business. During a reorganizational meeting, the officers of the company agreed to service the McArthur accounts and pay off his widow with the income derived from them. In return, we would receive various percentages of the company's stock. Kent Higgins, as president, received 50 per cent. I, with the title of executive vice president, received 18 per cent. And John MacKenzie, as vice president, was given 16 per cent. Finally, our versatile general manager and treasurer, George Moseley, also got 16 per cent.

By 1968, we had paid off most of the debt to Mrs. McArthur when an offer came from Longino & Porter, a competitor, for a merger — buyout deal. After much soul-searching and discussion, we agreed to their terms. Before paying off the balance owed Mrs. McArthur with the proceeds, we received approximately one million dollars. This amount included any income tax each individual would be required to pay. I remember my share was approximately $80,000 which was a hefty sum then, especially since it was tax free. The payments, which included accrued interest, were made over a period of five years.

Longino & Porter was owned by John Perry, a multi-millionaire who lived in West Palm Beach, Fla. Louis Sylvester, as executive vice president of Longino & Porter, had represented his firm in the negotiations and was placed in charge of the merged companies. The firm began operating under the unwieldy name of "Higgins-McArthur — Longino & Porter." Our name was placed first, it was explained to us, in order to benefit more from our reputation. This was soon shortened to "HM — L&P," an improvement, but still lacking in marketing value.

Louis Sylvester was a graduate of the esteemed Carnegie Tech school of printing, but he still lacked the managerial skills and leadership qualities to be a successful manager.

With the title of vice president, I continued servicing my accounts, but had little managerial authority. I determined to make the best of the situation and was successful in most of my endeavors. One plus — the new company had more sophisticated press equipment, which included two presses with five-color capability. This added a newer dimension to our sales efforts, making us more competitive.

In due course, Sylvester was replaced as manager by Jerry Marler, owner of another competing printing firm at the time he was hired by Mr. Perry. This meant a conflict of interest for Jerry, which was never explained. However, Jerry managed "by the book" and was successful.

The final manager Mr. Perry chose was an Englishman, Chris Evans, a long-time trouble-shooter for the Perry interests, especially at a daily newspaper publishing venture in Nassau. Chris was a competent businessman, having been a banker in England, and soon had the business operating more profitably, and he was generally popular with the employees.

With Chris Evans taking the helm, the firm's name was changed to "Perry Communications," which seemed to have a stimulating effect overall.

In the mid-eighties two Perry employees, Tommy Walker and John Simonton, joined with Dave Carley, III, an Atlanta banker, in an offer to buy the firm outright and operate it. Tommy, a former sales manager of the company, was the leader; Simonton, with a highly successful sales record; and Carley, with a strong financial background, completed the team of new owners after the successful buyout.

With the concurrence of Mr. Perry, the company continued to operate under the same name. Tommy Walker took the title of president, John Simonton, executive vice president, and Dave Carley, chief financial officer. These were people I knew well and felt comfortable working with. (Incidentally, Carley's father, Dave, Jr., former executive vice president of the First National Bank of Atlanta, was a good friend of mine before moving to Florida to continue his banking career.)

The operation went well for a few years under the new ownership. Then trouble struck with full force.

In January 1991, the doors of Perry Communications closed forever, leaving 93 employees idle — including me. The closure resulted from becoming over-extended and unable to meet its obligations. But Perry was not alone.

A story in the *Atlanta Business Chronicle*, dated March 11, 1991, said this in the opening paragraphs:

> The printing industry in Atlanta is staggering through a chapter in its history that it wishes had never been written. No business has escaped punishment from recession, but printing has been lashed particularly painfully. At least six smaller outfits in metro Atlanta involved in printing or pre-presswork... have closed their doors. So have two medium-size printing companies.

The story went on to report Perry as one of the companies closing because of "being unable to deal with heavy debt," and concluded with this statement: "How much longer this shake-out will continue is the question, and a matter of disagreement. Some printing executives take optimism from the outbreak of peace in the Middle East and predict the worst is past in their industry."

One printing company executive, who saw a "glimmer of hope," summed it up, "In all candor, there are a hell of a lot of printing companies in Atlanta, and really more than the city can stand."

Like most other Perry employees, I was surprised and stunned by the closing. Then I took stock. At age 75, I was determined to continue working as long as my health permitted, and the job held my interest. I was not wealthy, but, with social security, I had enough to live comfortably.

Then I received a call from Chip Clements, a former sales manager at Perry, who invited me to join him at Geographics, a reputable but lesser known firm south of Atlanta. I accepted his offer and began the long daily commute to their office and plant. But I was not happy working there among mostly strangers. Then, too, after printing a couple of issues, the Federal Reserve asked for bids on the *Economic Review* and I lost the contract. This was a blow, but I did retain *Parts Pups* and the annual Joke Book I had printed for years.

Deciding to leave Geographics, I approached friends at Stein Printing Company and made a deal to join them. This was done, of course, with the approval of Don Kite at Genuine Parts. At Stein, my job description was "outside contractor." I enjoyed my associations there, especially with long-time friend John Post, a salesman I had worked with at Perry.

After a couple of years, the lure of retirement became too strong to resist. Also, I felt compelled to finish writing my autobiography, especially pertaining to my military career, but also including my life before and after.

Thus ended my printing career spanning some 45 years.

WHAT INSPIRED AND MOTIVATED ME TO LIVE PAST 87

My life, except for the first 15 years, has spanned the entire 20th century, and extended well into the next. In my later years I have often wondered if I would reach and live beyond the new millennium.

A close friend of mine recently, without prompting, ascribed my longevity to two factors: Humor and sensible living habits. I would add a third and fourth — an excellent memory, even to this day, and the inheritance of good genes.

In the very first segment of this autobiography, I credited humor as being an important part of my 87-year existence. Throughout history, the literature of the ages has employed the balm of humor to provide a much-needed lighter note, and make reading more palatable.

Quotations from the writings of two well known English men of letters confirm my contention that spontaneous, uncontrived humor is best. One of these by Jonathan Swift, satirist and clergyman, who was born in Ireland, follows:

Humour is odd, grotesque, and wild,
Only by affectation spoil'd;
'Tis never by invention got,
Men have it when they know it not.
Jonathan Swift 1667 - 1745

The other following the same theme is this excerpt from the pen of Samuel Butler, novelist, essayist, and satirist:

The most perfect humour and irony is
generally quite unconscious.
Samuel Butler 1835 - 1902

Still further to the point is this personal reference: A longtime friend of mine, Mac McCoin, now living in Knoxville, Tenn., has informed me repeatedly that what I say is funniest when I am not attempting to be funny. (I'm still trying to decide if that's a compliment or not). Incidentally, Mac has written several highly readable novels and one is about to be published.

As for the sensible living habits I mentioned, these are just common sense rules for everyday life. I have consistently followed a regimen based on advice dispensed by every self-appointed fitness guru in the world today: Eat proper foods and exercise moderately on a regular basis.

My food fare is simple, consisting mostly of fresh fruits and vegetables, with very little meat. As for fitness, I have exercised for the past 15 years at least three days a week for an hour and a half each session.

A good memory can be both a blessing and a curse. It is gratifying to be able to recall past events clearly, but I find myself being repetitious and thus boring at times when recounting stories, especially humorous stories.

Above all, I give a fortunate inheritance of good genes, received from the grace of God, credit for whatever successes I have achieved in life.

A positive attitude means most in achieving success. Negative thoughts, I've found, hinder action and impede progress in any endeavor.

In some of the darkest, critical moments of my army career, at times when failure seemed inevitable, an inner surge of irrepressible strength and power came to the fore and sustained me. This reserve force seemed to surface at propitious moments.

This was especially true in some situations that demanded sound judgment, coupled with split-second decisions. Many examples of this are included in the segments of this book recounting my military experiences.

Both humble and proud describe my mixed feelings toward the "tribute" to me reproduced on the opposite page. Humble, because I do not feel worthy of such an outpouring of devotion and praise. Proud, because of being the recipient of so much unrestrained love and adoration from my youngest daughter, Lee Ann. And she's articulate, too. She tearfully presented me the eulogy in front of the entire assemblage at the family reunion on my 80th birthday at Myrtle Beach, South Carolina, in February 1985. Her references to some matters that may be obscure to the casual reader, I readily understand.

TRIBUTE

Father, thirty-seven years ago we became a family. The Lord gives us our earthly fathers to show His love, and He gave me the best one of all! You said I was your miracle baby and you always let me know I was special. Thank you for giving me a secure home, for always loving and supporting mother - I don't remember ever hearing you argue. You gave me a strong work ethic and showed me how to be honest and faithful. I remember sitting out in the back yard with you and mother on many a summer evening. It was a peaceful time and I was so happy. I still get that feeling when I hear the crickets chirping on summer nights.

Daddy, I'm so proud to be your daughter. You have always been a well-respected, well-liked man everywhere you have gone. Thank you for writing your book. It really helped me realize that you have feelings, struggles and questions just like I do. Forgive me for taking so long to see you as your own person and not just my daddy. Thank you for giving me a sense of history and roots.

Doda, you are so special to me. We would always go shopping for mother on Christmas Eve, just the two of us. You would dance with me when I was little and make me feel like a queen. I love you for your wonderful sense of humor - remember the side order of pancakes at Homosassa Springs? Thank you for taking me fishing and for all the wonderful vacations we had together. You gave me your time and attention - the things that let me know I'm important to you.

Now the Lord has given me a wonderful husband who is so much like you. And He has blessed us with a precious little boy. I'm so thankful for the opportunity for him to know his "Poopa". One day he will look back and be proud of the heritage you have left him, just as I am today.

With much love,
Lee ann

Feb. 10, 1995

In February of 1985, my entire clan gathered at Myrtle Beach, South Carolina, to celebrate my 80th birthday. Present were all three children and all of their progeny, including their spouses, children and grandchildren. Of these, two were my great grand-children. Pictured here is the entire group, with one notable exception — me, since I manned the camera. It is virtually impossible to identify here each individual in the photo, so I won't attempt to do so. Suffice it to say, we all had fun. I particularly enjoyed it.

On my 85th birthday, last February 14th, I was "surprised" by a bunch of my regular dining companions, plus three long-time lady friends and waitress Flo, at Mary Mac's, popular eatery in Midtown Atlanta. Many of us regulars, comprised of World War II veterans, meet there three times each week for a fun-filled luncheon. Humor is the keynote of the conversations, but we also swap lies and discuss our individual health problems in great detail. Most anyone is welcome, but a warning: Don't join us if you're allergic to healthful foods and stimulating conversation. It's difficult to identify everyone in the above picture due to space limitations of this caption, but names will be furnished upon request.

A Postmortem

REFLECTIONS ON LIFE BY AN OCTOGENARIAN

In a final effort to become more inspirational and motivational in my writing, I offer here some observations on a life spanning 87 years.

During the early morning hours of each day when my thoughts are most lucid, I better discern the motivational tugs that have propelled me forward.

Faith in one's self is all-important. You must believe in your ability to conquer — and deliver. Willingness to push forward and perform at your peak may be difficult, but it is nine-tenths of the battle. By putting your heart into it and exerting your utmost effort, you can and will succeed.

Once your accomplishments become the norm, they will be easier and easier. In fact, habitual, and thus second nature.

Consider each obstacle a test of your character. You will become stronger than you realize. Test yourself. You'll find this true.

Before the atomic bomb was dropped on Hiroshima, we were faced with losing up to one million casualties in a direct assault on the Japanese mainland. I could have been included in that number, if fate had so decreed.

Never strive to be a perfectionist. No human is perfect. You'll find solace in that fact, but don't use it as an excuse for failure. Always act decisively and cohesively to attain your goals.

These are words that would apply in any situation. You, too, can achieve as much with the right application of effort and energy. One famous test pilot called it "the right stuff." And you, too, have it, if you would just use it.

Attitude is the key. Gear yourself up to accomplish the impossible, and the impossible can become possible. You don't need to stay in the ranks of the ordinary. With persistence and determination, you can deliver a knockout blow to any obstacle in your path to success.

This is not intended to set myself up as a paragon to any degree. Several times I had close calls that threatened to change the even tenor of my life and lessen my self confidence. One such case in point: Because of a censorship mix-up, as recounted in "The Haugland Story" segment of this book, I was escorted to the office of General MacArthur by my two superior officers for possible reprimand and perhaps being relieved from my job as a censor. Fortunately, MacArthur decided in my favor, thus saving my job, as well as my reputation. If I had been removed, my whole life could have changed. I would have been branded a failure who couldn't hold his job, and might never have regained my prior stature, even in my own mind.

When the good Lord chooses to remove the last vestige of life from these mortal bones, I can honestly say I have had a full and mostly enjoyable life. And, hopefully, there's more in the offing.

A Vignette

MARGARET MITCHELL, GWTW... AND ME

After reading an advance copy of some of my book material, my granddaughter in Vermont, Lisa Cope, herself an accomplished writer and former weekly newspaper editor, gently chided me for failure to reveal that I had once known Margaret Mitchell and had attended the "Gone With the Wind" Ball in late 1939.

To correct that oversight and avoid being remiss (at least, in the eyes of Lisa), even though I originally thought it not interesting enough to record, here's my account of "knowing" Margaret Mitchell and attending the GWTW Ball:

In 1939, I happened to sit at a breakfast table next to Margaret Mitchell and her husband, John Marsh, during the annual Georgia Press Association Institute meeting in Athens. I also chatted with her, briefly and casually, at nightly cocktail parties at the old Georgian Hotel during the same meeting. My impression of her: very personable, but shy.

Although Margaret Mitchell did not choose to be present, I also attended the "Gone With the Wind" Ball held at the Atlanta City Auditorium in connection with the premiere. Here I almost rubbed elbows with Clark Gable, Vivien Leigh, Olivia de Havilland, and other celebrities, having been within a few feet of them — close enough to confirm that Clark Gable had big ears and Vivien Leigh was strikingly beautiful. They were readily accessible while mixing and mingling in the crowded auditorium. Contrary to rumor (which I may have started), I was not privileged to dance with Vivien Leigh.

I did not attend the premiere at Loew's Grand Theater, but I did see the movie there during the first week of its showing.

'WRITING FOR THE LUST OF IT'

T he intriguing title of this segment of my autobiography replicates the teacher's name for the best creative writing course I ever suffered through. I had always aspired to be a writer at some level, but that course became the catalyst that started my long-stilled creative juices flowing and bestirred in me the slumbering muse.

The teacher, Linda Clopton, an accomplished writer herself, still conducts classes in the Atlanta area. In fact, Linda taught several night courses I took, including one at Oglethorpe University and another at DeKalb County Community College. Just recently I received a mailing piece from Galloway School listing Linda's course in the night school classes at that institution. Reluctantly, I declined to attend, even though the school is just a short distance from my home.

The masthead of *Veranda* magazine lists Linda's day job as "Copy Editor/Writer." In that capacity, she works with some of the people I knew when *Southern Accents* was first published. One, Lisa Newcom, an assistant editor of the earlier magazine, founded *Veranda* and now serves as "Chairman/Editor-in-Chief." Another, Sims Bray, Jr., an advertising expert, has the title of "Publisher." From all indications, *Veranda* has become a leader in its field. Copies I see on the newsstand are bulging with advertising and filled with beautiful color photographs. Another indication of its success — it sells for $5.50 per copy.

During each class, Linda would lecture us on the finer points of good writing, then give us a subject and ask us to write a short piece on it within a given time period. She also gave us a subject for an assignment we were to write and bring to the next class the following week.

202 Edmund C. Hughes

One of these weekly subjects was, "Describe a safety pin." That was difficult to write, but here's the results of my efforts, which I happened to save:

> Safety Pin –
> A fastening device used to join and hold together two or more pieces of material.
> The safety pin is formed from a rigid, rounded thin strip of galvanized metal with a loop at its approximate center, which operates on a recoil principle, allowing it necesary flexibility of movement.
> A sharp-pointed, needle-like prong extends in one direction from the coiled loop. The other prong features a hooded fastener at its end.
> To utilize the fastener, the pointed end of one prong, after being inserted through the material to be joined, is forced into and held in place by the hooded clasp, thus providing the necessary restraining and holding capability.
> The safety pin, as the name connotes, has on occasion saved potential embarrassment to both the "pinner" and the "pinnee," especially during the early stages of the latter's life.

In critiquing our writings, Linda didn't spare the verbal whiplash. She was critical, but never harsh in her evaluations. Here's the gist of some her admonitions in 'Notes for Ed Hughes," dated 5/30/91:

— Look at each article and identify focus. Some of them seem to start off in one direction and end up in another.

— When doing flashbacks or flashforwards, be sure you segue so the reader doesn't get lost.

— Watch for parenthetical phrases. Often these can be put in separate sentences or even eliminated.

— Look for places where you might need to vary sentence structure.

— Try simplifying and using more active voice for variety and immediacy.

A modern day Hemingway would be hard put to follow her criteria to the letter. I could only exert a valiant effort in my learning process.

Endowed by nature with a vivid imagination, I have often cried out for the proper means of expressing myself. Thoughts can become elusive unless jotted down. During bursts of creativity, I find myself rising from my night-bed pillow to capture a word or phrase that had eluded me.

Unless recorded at once, these nuggets of thought can go "glimmering," as General MacArthur, at age 82, said to the cadets of West Point in referring to his "dreams of things that were." These fleeting nuggets of mine could thus be lost to posterity. This is said facetiously, of course, but such nighttime activity has caused me to suffer from sleep deprivation, and thus be inclined to grumpiness the next day. (My wife will readily attest to that.)

Another assignment Linda gave us was, "Mona Lisa - from the Waist Down." The subject matter, although questionable in taste, resulted in what I consider one of my best writing efforts. Why she chose such a subject remains a mystery. Anyway, I wrote the following, which I was required to read aloud in class:

> Mona Lisa - from the waist down
> "Paint faster, Leonardo. I'm freezing."
> Mona Lisa uttered these words as she impatiently waited for this modeling session to end. Just 10 more minutes to hold that enigmatic smile he wanted—in fact, insisted upon, until her face felt rigid from the cold.
> Right now in the early 16th century, it's tough being a model, she thought, sitting here in a drafty studio for a lousy 30 Liras an hour. She had held that certain facial expression for hours on end—literally on end, as the lower part of her body attested.
> A charcoal fire, smoldering in a small burner nearby, threw off but little heat.
> While resisting the cold, Mona Lisa sat stiffly upright with feet locked together. Her pudgy legs, covered with coarse black hair, protruded from a billowy skirt as she rested her crossed hands on one arm of the chair. Her

hands were small and dainty compared to other parts of her body.

Glancing up from his easel, Leonardo viewed hips appearing so large as to be grotesque, and buttocks that complely filled the bottom of the chair—with a slight overhang. Her skirt of loosely woven fabric did little to conceal flabby thighs.

Well-worn sandals adorned her feet and their lack of protection from the cold added to her misery.

"No wonder I'm so cold," she muttered. "I didn't put on my underpants."

If this borders on "writing for lust" in the worst sense, then so be it. In her critique, Linda wrote: "This is going nowhere," which was as stern a rebuke as she ever gave. At that point, I didn't want to go anywhere either, except home from that class and to bed.

My type of writing was sometimes termed "writing from the seat of the pants." That is, personal writing without a diary or journal to keep ideas in the proper context and corroborate facts and figures. I did keep a diary for a few weeks during my overseas army duty, but that stopped because of other demands on my time.

ABOUT THE AUTHOR

A 1937 journalism graduate of the University of Georgia, Edmund C. Hughes entered the newspaper field that same year as managing editor of a weekly, the *Cobb County Times*, in Marietta, Georgia. In 1938, that newspaper received national recognition, winning an unprecedented four first-place awards in competition sponsored by the National Editorial Association, including one for general excellence.

Through ROTC at Georgia, Hughes obtained a commission as a reserve second lieutenant and three years later was promoted to first lieutenant, just prior to being called to active duty on April 1, 1941. After serving for one year as a classification officer at the Reception Center at Fort Oglethorpe, Georgia, he was ordered to overseas duty on May 11, 1942.

Arriving in Australia on June 4, he was assigned shortly thereafter to the staff of General Douglas MacArthur as a public relations officer. He served in that capacity for almost three and a half years — from Melbourne to Tokyo — and was awarded the Bronze Star decoration in 1945 for "meritorious achievement in connection with military operations against the enemy in the Southwest Pacific Area from 5 July 1942 to 17 May 1945."

On September 2, 1945, Hughes witnessed the Japanese surrender ceremony aboard the battleship Missouri in Tokyo Bay.

Hughes left active service in October 1945 and entered the retired reserve with the rank of lieutenant colonel.

Following the war, he returned to Marietta and rejoined his pre-war employer, then as general manager of both the *Cobb County Times* and the publishing firm, Brumby Press. In that capacity, he directed the editorial policy of the newspaper and wrote a widely-read personal column each week. He held this position for five years before moving to Atlanta to join a leading printing establishment, Higgins-McArthur Company. Here he held several managerial posts before becoming executive vice-president in 1956 and acquiring part ownership of the firm.

Throughout this time, he attained many positions of leadership in both the printing industry and newspaper field, as well as in civic and charitable organizations.

He continued as a printing company executive during a series of mergers and acquisitions stemming from the original company. He retired in 1991.

Since retirement, besides completing his now being published autobiography titled "Living by the Seat of My Pants!," Hughes has engaged in compiling and editing books, mostly for friends and associates who have written their memoirs.

ISBN 155369458-9

9 781553 694588